❖ ANCIENT WORLD LEADERS ❖

NEFERTITI

◆ ◆ ◆

❖ ANCIENT WORLD LEADERS ❖

ALEXANDER THE GREAT

ATTILA THE HUN

CHARLEMAGNE

CLEOPATRA

CYRUS THE GREAT

DARIUS THE GREAT

GENGHIS KHAN

HAMMURABI

HANNIBAL

JULIUS CAESAR

KING DAVID

NEFERTITI

QUEEN OF SHEBA

RAMSES THE GREAT

SALADIN

XERXES

NEFERTITI

BRENDA LANGE

CHELSEA HOUSE
PUBLISHERS
An imprint of Infobase Publishing

Frontispiece: Bust of Queen Nefertiti. Circa 1350 B.C. Egypt, 18th Dynasty.

Nefertiti
Copyright © 2009 by Infobase Publishing

Chelsea House
An imprint of Infobase Publishing
132 West 31st Street
New York, NY 10001

Library of Congress Cataloging-in-Publication Data

Lange, Brenda.
  Nefertiti / Brenda Lange.
    p. cm. — (Ancient world leaders)
  Includes bibliographical references and index.
  ISBN 978-0-7910-9581-2 (hardcover)
  1. Nefertiti, Queen of Egypt, 14th cent. B.C.—Juvenile literature. 2. Egypt—History—Eighteenth dynasty, ca. 1570–1320 B.C.—Juvenile literature. 3. Queens—Egypt—Biography—Juvenile literature. I. Title. II. Series.
  DT87.45.L36 2008
  932'.014092—dc22   2008004869
  [B]

Text design by Lina Farinella
Cover design by Jooyoung An

Printed in the United States of America

Bang NMSG 10 9 8 7 6 5 4 3 2 1

This book is printed on acid-free paper.

❖ CONTENTS ❖

Foreword: On Leadership   6
Arthur M. Schlesinger, Jr.

1   The World of Nefertiti   12

2   Egypt Then and Now   23

3   Everyday Life in Ancient Egypt   33

4   Religion   47

5   Egyptian Royalty   59

6   The Lost City of Amarna
    and King Tut's Tomb   68

7   The Mysterious Queen Nefertiti   80

8   Could This Be Nefertiti?   90

Chronology   96
Bibliography   98
Further Reading   99
Photo Credits   100
Index   101
About the Authors   108

Arthur M. Schlesinger, Jr.

On Leadership

Leadership, it may be said, is really what makes the world go round. Love no doubt smoothes the passage; but love is a private transaction between consenting adults. Leadership is a public transaction with history. The idea of leadership affirms the capacity of individuals to move, inspire, and mobilize masses of people so that they act together in pursuit of an end. Sometimes leadership serves good purposes, sometimes bad; but whether the end is benign or evil, great leaders are those men and women who leave their personal stamp on history.

Now, the very concept of leadership implies the proposition that individuals can make a difference. This proposition has never been universally accepted. From classical times to the present day, eminent thinkers have regarded individuals as no more than the agents and pawns of larger forces, whether the gods and goddesses of the ancient world or, in the modern era, race, class, nation, the dialectic, the will of the people, the spirit of the times, history itself. Against such forces, the individual dwindles into insignificance.

So contends the thesis of historical determinism. Tolstoy's great novel *War and Peace* offers a famous statement of the case. Why, Tolstoy asked, did millions of men in the Napoleonic Wars, denying their human feelings and their common sense, move back and forth across Europe slaughtering their fellows? "The war," Tolstoy answered, "was bound to happen simply because it was bound to happen." All prior history determined it. As for leaders, they, Tolstoy said, "are but the labels that serve to give a name to an end and, like labels, they have the least possible connection with the event." The greater the leader, "the more conspicuous the inevitability and the predestination of every act he commits." The leader, said Tolstoy, is "the slave of history."

Determinism takes many forms. Marxism is the determinism of class. Nazism the determinism of race. But the idea of men and women as the slaves of history runs athwart the deepest human instincts. Rigid determinism abolishes the idea of human freedom—the assumption of free choice that underlies every move we make, every word we speak, every thought we think. It abolishes the idea of human responsibility, since it is manifestly unfair to reward or punish people for actions that are by definition beyond their control. No one can live consistently by any deterministic creed. The Marxist states prove this themselves by their extreme susceptibility to the cult of leadership.

More than that, history refutes the idea that individuals make no difference. In December 1931 a British politician crossing Fifth Avenue in New York City between 76th and 77th Streets around 10:30 p.m. looked in the wrong direction and was knocked down by an automobile— a moment, he later recalled, of a man aghast, a world aglare: "I do not understand why I was not broken like an eggshell or squashed like a gooseberry." Fourteen months later an American politician, sitting in an open car in Miami, Florida, was fired on by an assassin; the man beside him was hit. Those who believe that individuals make no difference to history might well ponder whether the next two decades would have been the same had Mario Constasino's car killed Winston Churchill in 1931 and Giuseppe Zangara's bullet killed Franklin Roosevelt in 1933. Suppose, in addition, that Lenin had died of typhus in Siberia in 1895 and that Hitler had been killed on the western front in 1916. What would the 20th century have looked like now?

For better or for worse, individuals do make a difference. "The notion that a people can run itself and its affairs anonymously," wrote the philosopher William James, "is now well known to be the silliest of absurdities. Mankind does nothing save through initiatives on the part of inventors, great or small, and imitation by the rest of us—these are the sole factors in human progress. Individuals of genius show the way, and set the patterns, which common people then adopt and follow."

Leadership, James suggests, means leadership in thought as well as in action. In the long run, leaders in thought may well make the greater difference to the world. "The ideas of economists and political philosophers, both when they are right and when they are wrong," wrote John Maynard Keynes, "are more powerful than is commonly understood. Indeed the world is ruled by little else. Practical men, who believe themselves to be quite exempt from any intellectual influences, are usually the slaves of some defunct economist. . . . The power of vested interests is vastly exaggerated compared with the gradual encroachment of ideas."

But, as Woodrow Wilson once said, "Those only are leaders of men, in the general eye, who lead in action. . . . It is at their hands that new thought gets its translation into the crude language of deeds." Leaders in thought often invent in solitude and obscurity, leaving to later generations the tasks of imitation. Leaders in action—the leaders portrayed in this series—have to be effective in their own time.

And they cannot be effective by themselves. They must act in response to the rhythms of their age. Their genius must be adapted, in a phrase from William James, "to the receptivities of the moment." Leaders are useless without followers. "There goes the mob," said the French politician, hearing a clamor in the streets. "I am their leader. I must follow them." Great leaders turn the inchoate emotions of the mob to purposes of their own. They seize on the opportunities of their time, the hopes, fears, frustrations, crises, potentialities. They succeed when events have prepared the way for them, when the community is awaiting to be aroused, when they can provide the clarifying and organizing ideas. Leadership completes the circuit between the individual and the mass and thereby alters history.

It may alter history for better or for worse. Leaders have been responsible for the most extravagant follies and most monstrous crimes that have beset suffering humanity. They have also been vital in such gains as humanity has made in individual freedom, religious and racial tolerance, social justice, and respect for human rights.

There is no sure way to tell in advance who is going to lead for good and who for evil. But a glance at the gallery of men and women in ANCIENT WORLD LEADERS suggests some useful tests.

One test is this: Do leaders lead by force or by persuasion? By command or by consent? Through most of history leadership was exercised by the divine right of authority. The duty of followers was to defer and to obey. "Theirs not to reason why/ Theirs but to do and die." On occasion, as with the so-called enlightened despots of the 18th century in Europe, absolutist leadership was animated by humane purposes. More often, absolutism nourished the passion for domination, land, gold, and conquest and resulted in tyranny.

The great revolution of modern times has been the revolution of equality. "Perhaps no form of government," wrote the British historian James Bryce in his study of the United States, *The American Commonwealth*, "needs great leaders so much as democracy." The idea that all people should be equal in their legal condition has undermined the old structure of authority, hierarchy, and deference. The revolution of equality has had two contrary effects on the nature of leadership. For equality, as Alexis de Tocqueville pointed out in his great study *Democracy in America*, might mean equality in servitude as well as equality in freedom.

"I know of only two methods of establishing equality in the political world," Tocqueville wrote. "Rights must be given to every citizen, or none at all to anyone . . . save one, who is the master of all." There was no middle ground "between the sovereignty of all and the absolute power of one man." In his astonishing prediction of 20th-century totalitarian dictatorship, Tocqueville explained how the revolution of equality could lead to the *Führerprinzip* and more terrible absolutism than the world had ever known.

But when rights are given to every citizen and the sovereignty of all is established, the problem of leadership takes a new form, becomes more exacting than ever before. It is easy to issue commands and enforce them by the rope and the stake, the concentration camp and the *gulag*. It is much harder to use argument and achievement to overcome opposition and win consent. The Founding Fathers of the United States understood the difficulty. They believed that history had given them the opportunity to decide, as Alexander Hamilton wrote in the first Federalist Paper, whether men are indeed capable of basing government on "reflection and choice, or whether they are forever destined to depend . . . on accident and force."

Government by reflection and choice called for a new style of leadership and a new quality of followership. It required leaders to be responsive to popular concerns, and it required followers to be active and informed participants in the process. Democracy does not eliminate emotion from politics; sometimes it fosters demagoguery; but it is confident that, as the greatest of democratic leaders put it, you cannot fool all of the people all of the time. It measures leadership by results and retires those who overreach or falter or fail.

It is true that in the long run despots are measured by results too. But they can postpone the day of judgment, sometimes indefinitely, and in the meantime they can do infinite harm. It is also true that democracy is no guarantee of virtue and intelligence in government, for the voice of the people is not necessarily the voice of God. But democracy, by assuring the right of opposition, offers built-in resistance to the evils inherent in absolutism. As the theologian Reinhold Niebuhr summed it up, "Man's capacity for justice makes democracy possible, but man's inclination to justice makes democracy necessary."

A second test for leadership is the end for which power is sought. When leaders have as their goal the supremacy of a master race or the promotion of totalitarian revolution or the acquisition and exploitation of colonies or the protection of greed and privilege or the preservation of personal power, it is likely that their leadership will do little to advance the cause of humanity. When their goal is the abolition of slavery, the liberation of women, the enlargement of opportunity for the poor and powerless, the extension of equal rights to racial minorities, the defense of the freedoms of expression and opposition, it is likely that their leadership will increase the sum of human liberty and welfare.

Leaders have done great harm to the world. They have also conferred great benefits. You will find both sorts in this series. Even "good" leaders must be regarded with a certain wariness. Leaders are not demigods; they put on their trousers one leg after another just like ordinary mortals. No leader is infallible, and every leader needs to be reminded of this at regular intervals. Irreverence irritates leaders but is their salvation. Unquestioning submission corrupts leaders and demeans followers. Making a cult of a leader is always a mistake. Fortunately, hero worship generates its own antidote. "Every hero," said Emerson, "becomes a bore at last."

The signal benefit the great leaders confer is to embolden the rest of us to live according to our own best selves, to be active, insistent, and resolute in affirming our own sense of things. For great leaders attest to the reality of human freedom against the supposed inevitabilities of history. And they attest to the wisdom and power that may lie within the most unlikely of us, which is why Abraham Lincoln remains the supreme example of great leadership. A great leader, said Emerson, exhibits new possibilities to all humanity. "We feed on genius. . . . Great men exist that there may be greater men."

Great leaders, in short, justify themselves by emancipating and empowering their followers. So humanity struggles to master its destiny, remembering with Alexis de Tocqueville: "It is true that around every man a fatal circle is traced beyond which he cannot pass; but within the wide verge of that circle he is powerful and free; as it is with man, so with communities." ◆

The World of Nefertiti

WHAT COMES TO MIND WHEN WE THINK ABOUT EGYPT? WE PICTURE THE vast Sahara Desert that covers much of northern Africa, where Egypt is located. We can see the Nile River—the longest in the world—that divides the country nearly in half, north to south. We think of people with a history that is long, mysterious, and beautiful. When we think of Ancient Egypt, we think of the pyramids, the Sphinx, and, of course, mummies. Yet, another item has come to symbolize the beauty of that mysterious land—the brightly painted bust of the lovely Queen Nefertiti.

Nefertiti's limestone sculpture is finely detailed and realistic. She holds her head with a royal grace, and her swanlike neck, high cheekbones, and full red lips remind of us of today's most beautiful supermodels. She wears a tall headdress of sky blue and a large necklace of long, gold beads known as *nefer* beads. Nefertiti's image has been reproduced countless times and has come to represent the ancient land and its people. We may feel as if we know the woman who posed for the artist thousands of years ago, but the little knowledge we do possess might have remained buried beneath the desert sand—along with the bust—if not for a fortuitous accident in 1912.

That year, a team of German archaeologists uncovered the city of Amarna, located almost in the center of the country, on the east bank of the Nile River. Amarna had been built by Nefertiti's husband, the Pharaoh (or King) Akhenaten, as a tribute to the sun-disk god, Aten. In 1912, a poor woman happened upon some buried pottery and alerted the authorities. The artifacts—including many images of Nefertiti and her family—uncovered at this site added greatly to the world's treasure trove of knowledge. In fact, it is considered one of the most valuable finds of Ancient Egypt because it has educated us about a period in Egyptian history that was previously shrouded in mystery. Its treasures were remarkably well preserved, in part because—soon after Akhenaten's death—Amarna was abandoned, partially destroyed, and left to be buried under the desert sands. It was never resettled, so everything found there came from the approximately 20-year period it was inhabited by the Pharaoh Akhenaten, his Queen Nefertiti, and about 20,000 subjects.

TIME FRAME

We separate Ancient Egypt into three separate kingdoms, with three intermediate periods between each kingdom. (The precise dates given to these eras vary somewhat, depending on which scholar you read.) During this time, 30 dynasties—or families—ruled the country. Remember that B.C., or the years before the birth of Jesus Christ, are counted backward: the lower the date, the closer to our present time. After the death of Christ, or A.D., the dates follow the pattern we are familiar with today. The Old

Nefertiti and her husband Akhenaten ruled Egypt during the New Kingdom, in a period known as Amarna. Although her husband was the all-powerful pharaoh, fascination over Nefertiti has made her the better-known monarch. These limestone figures of Nefertiti and Akhenaten date from the Amarna period.

Kingdom existed from about 2686 to 2160 B.C. and included the third through sixth dynasties. This era was characterized by pharaohs who wielded nearly complete power over their people and were considered gods as well as kings. The Pharaoh Djoser was one of the more well-known kings to reign during this time, which is sometimes called "the Age of the Pyramids" because of the many tombs built within the pyramids. Djoser is known for the famous step pyramid he built for his tomb. The Pharaoh Khufu also ruled, during the fourth dynasty; he is known for building the Great Pyramid at Giza. The capital of Egypt was located in Memphis during this period.

The Middle Kingdom lasted from about 2055 to 1650 B.C.; it began during the eleventh dynasty and ended toward the close of the thirteenth. Pharaohs held slightly less control than in the previous era, although government continued pretty much as it had earlier. Priests and local officials grew in power and prestige. Fewer large monuments were built, and agriculture increased along the Nile.

The New Kingdom—the era that includes the Amarna Period—lasted from about 1570 to 1070 B.C., and it included the eighteenth through twentieth dynasties. This time period was host to some of the most well-known pharaohs, including Nefertiti, who ruled with her husband during the eighteenth dynasty. Other famous names from the New Kingdom include Tutenkhamen, Seti, and Ramses. Priests and other officials retained their significant power, and trade was strong. The country prospered.

Ancient Egypt was divided into upper and lower regions; it was not united as one country until approximately 3400 B.C., when a powerful pharaoh united the two areas. Following the end of the New Kingdom, the country was ruled in part by a succession of foreign powers, including the Persians, Greeks, and Romans, and finally came under Islamic rule around 700 A.D. During the 1500s, Egypt was ruled by the Ottoman Turks, who maintained rule for nearly 300 years. Napoleon invaded from France in 1798. Egypt gained its independence from Great Britain in 1922. Today, the country is a republic, and Mohammed Hosni Mubarak has served as president since October 1981. The country is home to nearly 80 million people, most of whom still make their living near the banks of the Nile River.

Many famous pharaohs ruled during the early centuries, and still others are barely remembered by history. Some ruled for only a few years; some took the throne as young boys and held onto their power until they were very old. It was rare for women to hold much power in Ancient Egypt, but a few females were great influences on the pharaohs (whether their husbands or sons); in these cases, the women were the power behind the throne. Several women were pharaohs in their own right. Nefertiti may have been one of the rarest of Egyptian women: one who first had great influence over the king, and who then ruled as pharaoh following the king's death.

HOW POWERFUL WAS NEFERTITI?

There is a lot of speculation about exactly how much influence Nefertiti actually had. Because so many paintings, sculptures, and reliefs show her in a position of power—including making offerings to Aten, the sun-disk god—it is presumed that she was actually quite influential. Some Egyptologists—scientists who study Ancient Egypt—believe that she died about three years before Akhenaten did, because there is no mention of her in records after that time. Others point to the emergence of someone named Smenkhkare, who ruled as co-regent (coruler) with Akhenaten's son, Tutenkhamen, and then disappeared—leaving King Tut, as Tutenkhamen is more commonly known, to rule on his own. Because Nefertiti's tomb has never been identified conclusively, we may never really know whose theories are correct.

It was quite common for a ruler to appoint his successor while he was still alive. This gave the ruling pharaoh a chance to prepare the next king for the responsibilities he would someday inherit. Generally, rule passed from father to son. Sometimes this lineage could get confusing, because kings often had several wives with whom they had children. In the case of Akhenaten, Nefertiti was his primary wife; however, because the couple had only daughters, it was up to one of the secondary wives, Kiya, to provide Akhenaten with an heir. Tutenkhamen, one of Ancient Egypt's most celebrated pharaohs, was this son and heir.

Akhenaten reigned for 17 years in the latter part of the eighteenth dynasty, from 1350 to 1334. Early in his reign, he moved the capital city north—from Thebes to Amarna—and built a new capitol there. The next two decades are commonly known as the Amarna Period, after this new city. This period became one of the most controversial times in Ancient Egyptian history because of the changes in religion and art that Akhenaten and Nefertiti instituted.

EGYPTIAN RELIGIOUS PRACTICES

The Ancient Egyptians practiced *polytheism*, or the worship of more than one god. In fact, they had hundreds of gods. Some gods we might recognize, such as Osiris, the god of life, death, and fertility; his wife, Isis, goddess of the throne; their son, Horus, the god who allowed pharaohs to become godlike; and his brother Set, the god of the desert. Egyptians prayed to their gods and goddesses for everything. They prayed to one god to raise the level of the Nile just enough to create the fertile farmland they required, and they prayed to another god to give them an abundant harvest. If they felt the gods were unhappy because the crops were poor or disease had struck the population, priests might make sacrifices of a sheep, cow, or duck. Every part of the Egyptians' lives was governed by their religious beliefs and the whims of their gods and goddesses.

NEFERTITI AND AKHENATEN MAKE CHANGES

Soon after he was crowned, Akhenaten ordered the people to worship only one god, Aten. In pictures, Aten is depicted as a round sun disk, with long rays ending in hands that hold an

ankh, the hieroglyphic symbol for life. Previously, all gods had
been depicted as animals, or as half animal, half human. Aten's
different appearance was one of several changes caused by the
worship of this new god. In the old religion, several priests
were required to care for each deity. The people had no direct
contact with their gods; instead, the priests and assistant priests
served as intermediaries, speaking to the gods and interpreting
their needs. This authority gave the priests enormous control
over their people, and they lived comfortable lives of prestige
and power. Under Akhenaten's worship of Aten, however, there
were no priests to intervene, and the priests were not happy
about their loss of power. Akhenaten was the only connection
to the god, making him somewhat of a god himself. Aten was
not a new god, though. The sun-disk symbol had always been a
part of the worship of the sun god, Ra. Yet the notion of sepa-
rating the disk from the main deity was never considered until
Akhenaten introduced it.

Akhenaten and Nefertiti did not just revolutionize the way
the people worshiped. They also demanded that artists and
sculptors take a new view of the world. Artists of the Amarna
Period were encouraged to portray their surroundings realisti-
cally instead of in the highly stylized and impressionistic manner
of previous artists. Kings and queens always had been pictured
in paintings and other works of art as regal and godlike. Yet
Akhenaten and Nefertiti were portrayed as an affectionate and
very human couple, holding hands and playing with their children. The paintings, sculptures, and reliefs that survived from
the time of the eighteenth dynasty are quite distinctive and easily recognizable, because the subjects in them have features that
are much more human.

Some of Akhenaten's subjects remained loyal and went along
with all of these changes unquestioningly, perhaps to remain in
the king's good favor. Others, however, refused to change what
they had always believed and how they had always lived just
because the pharaoh said to do so. Despite Akhenaten's decree

When Akhenaten took the throne, the new pharaoh rescinded some of the power given to Egyptian priests and declared Aten, the sun god, the only deity worthy of worship. Aten was symbolized as a sun disk, with his rays beaming over people, as in this painted limestone depicting Akhenaten, Nefertiti, and three of their daughters sitting beneath Aten.

to worship only Aten, religious symbols, drawings, and writings have been found in other parts of Egypt—dating to the Amarna Period—that had nothing to do with Aten. Changes are not always welcome, and apparently many of the changes demanded by the royal couple were unpopular and only confused and angered many Egyptian people.

In Amarna, Akhenaten and Nefertiti built palaces and a temple to Aten; there, they were joined there by family and those people who worshiped Aten along with them. Yet, Amarna did not last long: It rose, thrived, and fell within about 20 to 25 years. Several years after Akhenaten's death, Egyptian priests and people rebelled against monotheistic (worship of one god) society and went back to their old ways. Eventually, evidence of Amarna was destroyed, and most of Aten's temples and Akhenaten's palaces were obliterated. Many references to Aten—and to Akhenaten and Nefertiti—were erased or written over. The desert sands eventually covered the ruins of the city, and they remained hidden until their discovery in 1912. Because no other cities were built on that site, the objects found there leave a clear record of life during Akhenaten's reign, as well as that of his son Tutankhamen. Scholars believe that so much was left behind, relatively intact, because it was considered worthless.

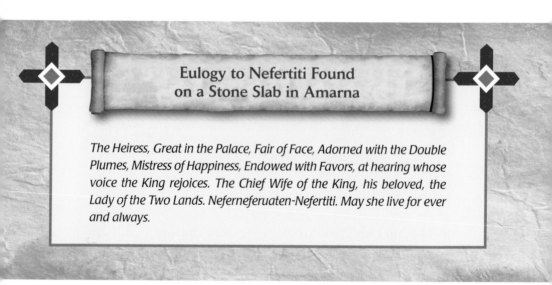

Eulogy to Nefertiti Found on a Stone Slab in Amarna

The Heiress, Great in the Palace, Fair of Face, Adorned with the Double Plumes, Mistress of Happiness, Endowed with Favors, at hearing whose voice the King rejoices. The Chief Wife of the King, his beloved, the Lady of the Two Lands. Neferneferuaten-Nefertiti. May she live for ever and always.

MYSTERIOUS ICON

Nefertiti remains very much an object of mystery, even though she is one of the icons of Egyptian history. Little is known of her life before she married Akhenaten, or even of her life during her marriage. Drawings and sculptures found at Amarna, along with writings of ancient scribes, provide the extent of our knowledge. Some Egyptologists theorize that Nefertiti came to Egypt from another country, because her name means "the beautiful woman has come." Her long neck and full lips may suggest a different ethnicity. Others believe that she was a commoner by birth—the daughter of a court official—and her beauty caught the king's eye. Still others think that she was of royal blood. We do know that she was Akhenaten's primary wife, and as such wielded great power at court. Most Egyptian men married only one woman at a time, but *polygamy* (marriage to more than one spouse at a time) was common among royalty. It is believed that Akhenaten had three or four wives and at least eight children—six girls with Nefertiti, and two boys by two other wives.

Nefertiti's bust has become nearly as familiar as the painting of the Mona Lisa, and both share the same sort of mystique. Nefertiti is widely regarded as one of the most beautiful women in antiquity, even though the left eye is missing from the bust. The limestone bust is extremely realistic; it contains fine detail, including tiny lines around the eyes, mouth, and neck. Scientists believe that the bust originally was meant as a sculptor's model for his students, which is why one eye was missing—to demonstrate the sculpting of the eye socket. More likely, it was the model for the official royal portrait of the queen. Both of these explanations are plausible, because the bust was found in the ruins of the official court sculptor, Thutmose. The limestone retained the bright hues used to color her skin, lips, headdress, and elaborate necklace, and its burial in the dry desert sands preserved this beautiful woman for posterity.

There is much that we may never know about Nefertiti and her origins, her controversial husband, their relatively brief reign, and her death. Theories and possibilities abound but will likely remain unproven. Yet, thanks to the first discoveries at Amarna—and the ongoing excavations there and elsewhere in Egypt—we can construct a fairly accurate picture of what life was like in the late eighteenth dynasty, during the rule of Akhenaten and Nefertiti in the land of the kings.

2

Egypt Then and Now

EGYPT IS A LAND OF MYSTERY. ANCIENT RUINS AND GRAVESITES, PAINTINGS and strange symbols, myths, tales, and thousands of years of history awaken the sleuth in all of us. We want to know more about the country's people and how they lived. *Egyptology*, or the study of that country and its history, has become quite popular. Many books have been written and documentaries produced that explore the pharaohs, pyramids, and other antiquities. Movies about Cleopatra, King Tut's tomb, and the recent Discovery Channel documentary about Nefertiti seek to inform us as much as they leave us wondering about this time and its people. We tend to think we know a lot about Ancient Egypt, but much about its ancient people is speculation. Before going back in time to try to figure them out, it helps to know something about the country today: where it is located, its land and climate, and a little bit about modern Egyptian society.

THE LAND

Egypt is located in the northeastern corner of Africa and covers nearly 370,000 square miles. It is bordered to the west by Libya, to the south by Sudan, and to the north and east by the Mediterranean and Red seas, respectively. The land is divided by the Nile River, which flows north from central Africa and empties into the Mediterranean Sea more than 4,100 miles later. The Nile, the world's longest river, ranges from 1 to 12 miles wide, with tributaries branching off. Where the Nile reaches the Mediterranean Sea, it fans out and enters the sea by way of several mouths. This area is known as the Nile River delta. Every year, the Nile floods when heavy rainfall at the higher elevations in Ethiopia fills the river and overflows its banks. This annual inundation is vital to Egyptian farmers, who rely on the dark, nutrient-rich soil left behind to help them grow abundant crops. Floods occur between June or July and September or October, and crops are planted as floodwaters recede.

The country has two seasons. The hot season lasts from May to October, with temperatures reaching up to 126° Fahrenheit (52° Celsius) in the daytime. From November to April, or the cool season, temperatures drop to between 55° and 70° Fahrenheit (13°–21°C). Green fields rich with crops and grasses join swaying palm trees along the Nile's banks, where soil is rich and water is plentiful. Wildlife is plentiful too. Camels, horses, water buffalo, snakes, lizards, and millions of birds populate the country. Today, cranes and herons—which recently have become endangered—are protected by the government. Lotus and papyrus plants are plentiful in the Nile River delta. Throughout the desert, where springs bubble to the surface, oases are formed that also harbor various plant life. If you look at aerial photographs of Egypt, the delta area is a green "V" shape, where crops and vegetation can grow because of the annual flooding and subsequent irrigation by Egypt's farmers. The dividing line between green abundance and tan desert is sharp.

THE PEOPLE

For about 3,000 years, the land was ruled by a succession of pharaohs. Through 30 dynasties, the Ancient Egyptians lived, worked, worshiped, and left a multitude of artifacts behind. Persians occupied the country from approximately 525 to 332 B.C. Although they allowed the Egyptian people to live much as they had prior to their occupation, rebellion was rampant and people rejoiced when Alexander the Great invaded the country (approximately 333 B.C.). Nearly 300 years later, just after the reign of the famous Queen Cleopatra VII, Egypt was ruled by a succession of foreign countries that included the Romans, Arabs, and Turks. Egypt became part of the British Empire around 1700 and gained full independence in 1952, declaring Gamal Abdel Nasser—leader of the revolution—as its president. Hosni Mubarak has been the president of the republic since 1981.

More than 250,000 years ago, when the first inhabitants made their way to Egypt, grasslands covered the countryside. Scientists believe that, sometime near 25,000 B.C., the climate began to change, turning the verdant fields into bare deserts with shifting sand dunes. In approximately 3400 B.C., settlers from Iraq moved onto the lands around the banks of the Nile and built villages of mud huts there and in desert oases. These immigrants raised cattle and grew wheat and barley in the dark soil along the Nile. Each year—after the river's floodwaters receded—the farming year began, with men making full use of the rich silt left behind. Simple tools of wood and flint were used to cut the wheat and separate the grain from the chaff. Long canals served to irrigate distant fields. Men filled the canals using river water the same way they do today, with a device called a *shaduf*—a pole supported by a trellis with a weight at one end. The arm is easily raised and lowered by one person, filling bucket after bucket, which is emptied into the canal. The areas served by the irrigation ditches were green and fertile. The line between this area and the desert—where the ditches end—is stark, as was the difference between life and death for the Egyptians. Farming was a critical part of life in Ancient Egypt, with most people involved in one way or another to help produce adequate crops.

More than half of today's Egyptians still live in rural areas, where agriculture remains the way of life. Just as their ancestors did thousands of years ago, today's rural Egyptians farm the land and raise sheep, cattle, and goats. Their food is a mix of Turkish, Greek, Palestinian, Lebanese, and Syrian influences. Lunch is their main daily meal; it consists of bread (similar to pita bread), *foul* (boiled fava beans), and *t'miya* (fried balls of chickpeas and wheat). Puddings and sweet cakes are served for dessert. Arabic is the official language, and many different dialects are found throughout the country.

ANCIENT TIMES

The Nile was at the heart of the lives of the Ancient Egyptians—about one million of them, spread across approximately 12,500 square miles. The land has been called the "greatest oasis" and is known as the cradle of Egyptian civilization. Although Egypt was one country, it was divided into two segments, known as Upper Egypt (which, despite its name, lay in the southern part of the country) and Lower Egypt (which lay in the north). The dividing line was roughly where Cairo, the capital, is located today. Each part of the country had its own symbols, and the kings wore different crowns. Later, the pharaoh would wear a crown that used parts of both crowns—the tall, white, hat-like crown of Upper Egypt combined with the lower, flatter, red crown of Lower Egypt.

In ancient times, people lived in clusters along the banks of the Nile. Most of the Egyptians were farmers who relied on the annual flooding of the river to help create perfect conditions

Because most of Egypt was desert, irrigation methods were quickly developed to help sustain the kingdom. The shaduf *(above, in foreground)* was a simple mechanism used to lift buckets of water out of the Nile and into the fields. Almost 20 liters of water were needed in order to irrigate one square meter of land for one day.

for farming. Higher elevations received a great deal of rainfall, which ran through the Nile and normally flooded the river valley for several weeks during the summer months. What was left behind when the floodwaters receded was a dark soil—rich in nutrients—that created the perfect, fertile environment for crops to flourish. This land was called the *black land*. The vast Sahara Desert, which covers much of northern Africa, lies to the west of the river, and mountains border the eastern desert along the Red Sea coast. The desert, in which nothing could survive, was known as the red land. Crops were usually planted in October and harvested in March or April. The mountainous eastern desert was divided by dry riverbeds called *wadis* that became trade routes across the desert to the Red Sea. These natural elements created excellent barriers against would-be invaders. The Nile River also helped keep the country more or less isolated, due to its many rapids south of Egypt and dense marshes to the north. This semi-isolation helped form Ancient Egypt's unique culture.

Birds were everywhere, attracted by the abundant fish in the river and the fields of wheat. Pintail ducks, cormorants, pelicans, geese, and hoopoes all called the Nile River delta home. Lions, wild bulls, antelopes, gazelles, hyenas, and jackals lived in the desert. The ancient people domesticated donkeys, camels, cows, and sheep and kept cats as pets. In fact, cats were considered sacred and often were mummified and buried alongside their masters to keep them company in the afterlife. Sometimes, little faces were painted on the linen bandages used to cover their bodies. The mummified cats were dedicated to the Goddess Bastet, who was depicted as a woman with the head of a cat. Egypt was home to several relatively safe wild animals, such as ducks, geese, gazelles, frogs, and camels, but the people were wary of the two most dangerous river beasts at the time (and perhaps now, as well): hippos and crocodiles.

SCULPTURES AND OTHER GREAT WORKS OF ART

Egypt is full of imposing, carved stone sculptures that everyone identifies with that country. One of its classic symbols of both the ancient and modern world is the Sphinx. This 150-foot-long limestone structure has the body of a lion and the head of a king or god, and it was carved about 4,500 years ago. Most

Egyptologists believe that the Great Sphinx was carved with the face of the Pharoah Khafre, whose tomb it "guards."

The Great Pyramid of Giza is one of the seven wonders of the ancient world and stands near the Sphinx on the outskirts of the city of Giza, several miles from Cairo in the northern part of the country. The elaborately designed pyramid was built as the tomb of King Khufu around 2540 B.C. Today's scientists still are not completely sure how the builders were able to construct it. They believe that slaves and other workers toiled constantly for at least 20 years, painstakingly placing each of the 2.3 million limestone blocks that weigh an average of one ton each. Another pyramid was built for King Djoser about 100 years later; it is called the Step Pyramid for the way the blocks are placed in steps going up toward the peak. These steps were supposed to represent the staircase the king would climb after death to join the sun god.

Pyramid is a Greek word meaning "place of ascension." Limestone, sandstone, and granite used to build many of the

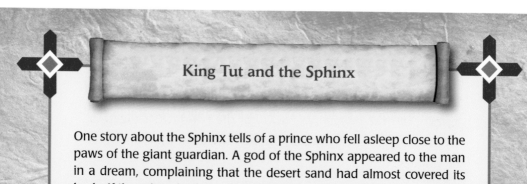

King Tut and the Sphinx

One story about the Sphinx tells of a prince who fell asleep close to the paws of the giant guardian. A god of the Sphinx appeared to the man in a dream, complaining that the desert sand had almost covered its body. If the prince had the sand cleared away, the Sphinx promised he would become the ruler of Egypt. This young man did as he was asked and later became King Thutmose IV. The shifting desert sands have nearly covered the structure many times, and they have been cleared away many times as well.

tombs and temples came from the hills on the edge of the river. The river also was used as a highway to transport these building materials north and south. Pharaohs and their families were buried in this area throughout the Old and Middle kingdoms. Scientists are unsure why rulers of the New Kingdom began building their tombs in the hills around the Valley of the Kings near modern-day Luxor, but they speculate it was to elude tomb robbers, who knew they would find great riches when they raided the pyramids.

The Ancient Egyptians are well known for their appreciation of beautiful artwork. They used painting and sculpting to express their love of life, to worship their gods, and to depict scenes from everyday life. Paintings and drawings were impressionistic and followed strict guidelines. Human figures were stiff and formal. They were always shown with their bodies facing forward and their heads turned to one side, so they were seen partly from the front and partly in profile. Men and women usually were depicted as young and beautiful; pictures of old age and sickness were rare, although images do exist of people with crutches or without sight. In temples, paintings and reliefs (when the image is carved deeply into stone) might show royals and gods; in tombs, they might show men fishing or farming. Usually, the bigger the figure or scene depicted, the more important the subject. The Ancient Egyptians appreciated beautiful objects, so there are many paintings of natural beauty and elaborate carvings.

KARNAK

Karnak is a massive city of temples and shrines, built over more than a thousand years. It was dedicated to the king of the gods, Amun-Ra, and served as a center of religious life and culture. The complex is located about two miles north of Luxor (the ancient city of Thebes) and is more than two miles around. It contains some of the most impressive architecture in Egypt.

The Great Sphinx, one of Egypt's most recognizable symbols, was built almost 4,500 years ago. Although in fairly good condition, the Sphinx has undergone restoration treatments throughout the years to preserve what is left of the great monument. It is believed the statue once featured a plaited beard, a cobra in the middle of its forehead, and a nose.

The fact that this combination of temples and other buildings was built over such a long period of time, and by so many different pharaohs (30 in all), lends it a unique diversity. Statues, huge columns covered with hieroglyphs, and two of the only surviving obelisks from antiquity are some of the impressive finds in Karnak.

THE VALLEY OF THE KINGS

A large valley on the western shores of the Nile River in southern Egypt, across from the city of Thebes (now Luxor), is known as the Valley of the Kings. Many pharaohs and nobles (as well as wives and children)—primarily from the New Kingdom dynasties (the eighteenth through twentieth)—were buried in the hills surrounding the valley. This is where the tomb of King Tut was discovered in 1922 and where many archeological digs continue today. Sixty-four separate tombs have been identified in the valley and are known as KV1, KV2, and so on. The KV stands for "Kings' Valley." KV1 is the tomb of Ramses VI, who reigned from 1133 to 1125 B.C. and was the sixth king of the twentieth dynasty. His tomb was opened thousands of years ago but only completely excavated in the mid-1980s. KV63 was unearthed in May 2005, and seven coffins and clay jars were found inside. No bodies were found, but materials for mummification, including linens, salt, and pottery, were discovered. Egyptologists believe this was a storage chamber and not a tomb. KV64 is not yet proven to be a tomb at all; it is seen on radar as an underground room or cavern of some sort.

No burial chamber has ever been discovered for Queen Nefertiti, although there is speculation that one of three mummies in a side chamber in one of the valley's tombs may be that of the queen. Various Egyptologists believe that this mummy can only be Nefertiti, based on circumstantial evidence; however, based on that same evidence, others believe that it is not her.

Ultimately, time and the elements may have chipped away at some of the original Egyptian stonework, but wonder and awe at the builders' accomplishments have not been eroded.

3

Everyday Life in Ancient Egypt

FOR ALL ITS DIFFICULTIES, LIFE IN ANCIENT EGYPT WAS ORDERLY AND could be quite full and happy. Of course, if you were born into royalty, your life was much different—and easier—than that of the large middle class, and obviously much easier than the lives of the slaves. There also was much that bound all the people together—a love of family, religion, beauty, art, and culture. At the top of the social order were the royals—pharaohs and their wives and children. The upper class consisted of priests, noblemen, officials, and scribes. Many of the members of this class lived at court, or in the several palaces maintained by the royal family. The middle class was large and comprised the artists, craftsmen, soldiers, and teachers. Farmers, servants, and other workers made up the lower class, and slaves—who usually were captured foreign soldiers and sometimes their families—were the lowest class.

FAMILY LIFE

The Ancient Egyptians celebrated family life. Often, several generations lived together under one roof and, because lives were often cut short by disease or accident, cared for one another regardless of family relationships. In other words, many children were raised by grandparents or other relatives if their father was killed or their mother died in childbirth. Children were regarded as great blessings. If a couple could not have children, they often said special prayers and made tributes to the gods that they would conceive. They might even pray to dead relatives to intervene with the gods to give them children. Sometimes these couples might adopt. Most families were large and included four, five, or more children. In part, women had so many children because of the high rate of infant mortality. About 25 percent of babies died before they reached their first birthday, and another 50 percent of all children died before they turned 10. Diseases that we think of as minor today, or those that can be fought with our modern medicines—such as intestinal infections—were killers in Ancient Egypt, when medicine was much more primitive and relied heavily on magic.

Men and women and boys and girls held what we consider "traditional" roles. The women would cook and bake and tend to the home and children, and they taught their daughters these skills. Even though the women were expected to obey their husbands and fathers, they had fairly equal legal standing. Women were allowed to own their own land and conduct business. They were not permitted to become scribes, but neither were they considered second-class citizens. When a woman married, she was given a certain amount of cash or belongings with which to help set up the new household. If the couple were to divorce, she would take the same amount with her. A young girl generally did not receive a formal education of any sort, but instead learned everything she needed to know from her mother or another female relative. When a boy married, he usually moved into the family home with his new wife.

The men primarily were farmers and worked hard to raise crops and livestock to provide food for their families. These farmers also were required to help build temples and tombs during the time of the annual flooding of the Nile, when they were unable to farm. It is believed that this national service requirement helped get the great pyramids built. These farmers—along with slaves—pitched in to create the great monuments in the desert. Other men were trained as craftsmen or artisans and worked with stone and wood to create furniture, boats, and tools. Artists also were skilled in metalworking; they created beautiful jewelry, hair ornaments, and other items from glass, gold, silver, precious jewels, and pewter. Potters also were in high demand for their carved figures, and for pottery made from clay and silt from the Nile. Talented woodworkers carved everything from toys and furniture to ships from native trees—such as the juniper, acacia, and palm—or from imported woods that included cedar and ebony. The skills of these craftsmen were appreciated and rewarded by kings and queens, and the artisans proudly taught their sons the trade, keeping the family's traditions intact.

Generations lived together, and the young people cared for their elders. When the parents died, the sons would inherit any land they had owned, and the daughters would inherit the household belongings. Marriages sometimes were prearranged (but often not) and took place at a very young age, usually about 12 or 13, because 40 years was the average life span. There was no formal marriage ceremony; a couple would just set up a household together as proof of commitment to their union. Although the king could have several wives, ordinary men had just one wife at a time. Divorce was possible, although it was uncommon. In the case of divorce, as mentioned previously, the

Life in Ancient Egypt was not easy for ordinary citizens who were not of nobility or royalty. Farmers who did not own their own land paid landowners with part of their crop, while some slaves *(above)* were forced to serve upper-class families. Both farmers and slaves were expected to help with the building of the pyramids.

wife was allowed to keep any material belongings she had had when she married, including any land.

Education in Ancient Egypt generally consisted of what was taught to children by their parents or other guardians. Children would learn about their religion and the world around them by example and by stories passed down through the generations. Children also learned to obey a certain moral code, in which they were taught not to lie, cheat, steal, and so on. These teachings helped the people maintain the sense of order and balance that was so important to them. More formal schooling was reserved for boys of the upper class—who would become scribes, priests, or government officials—because it was expensive. Middle- and lower-class boys and girls were needed to help their families farm, work at crafts, and run the house. Those boys who did receive a formal education were taught by priests in temple schools. There were no textbooks. Students learned how to write by practicing on pieces of limestone, pottery, or boards, and other lessons were recited. Paper was too precious to use on schoolchildren. Reeds with frayed ends, dipped in ink, were used as brushes. Mathematics, history, astronomy, and geography were common subjects.

Just like children today, young Egyptians loved to play outdoors. They played leapfrog, tug-of-war, board games, and ball games; played with dolls and toy animals; and did spinning dances. Stories revolved around experiences of everyday life. One story about a wax toy crocodile that comes to life when thrown into the river was meant to remind the young that crocodiles were a very real threat. Balls were filled with small seeds to make baby rattles. A board game called "Snake" was popular; shaped like a coiled snake with an eye in the center, it was set up much like Parcheesi. Players moved counters around the circle, and the first one to arrive at the eye was the winner. Many examples of these games and toys have been found in excellent condition among the ruins of Ancient Egypt. Tomb paintings show children at play and adults relaxing with board games during various celebrations.

Differences between the middle class and nobility were obvious. Quality of food, types of entertainment, forms of housing, and styles of dress all served to separate the classes.

Of course, the rich had the finest linen to wear and place on their beds, whereas that of the poor was coarse (and probably itchy). The rich ate more meat and had servants to prepare their meals, and they were often entertained by singers and dancing girls at lavish dinner parties. The poor ate a lot of bread as well as vegetables and fruit that they grew themselves. Beer made from barley wheat was a common beverage for all classes.

Daily activities were remarkably similar. Women ran the household, although rich women had servants to help with the chores and the children, and those who had no servants spent a lot of time grinding wheat and baking bread. Lower-class men spent their days toiling in the fields or working at their crafts, while upper-class men would visit their farm fields to ensure that their workers were doing their jobs.

MEDICINE

Although ancient medicine was a mix of scientific observation and magic, Egyptian doctors could be quite skilled. They had medicines to treat many different common diseases, which they believed were caused by tiny creatures. Egyptologists believe that Ancient Egyptians suffered from many intestinal ailments due to parasites in their water and meat. They probably had many problems with their eyes as well, because of the blowing desert sands and the bright sunlight.

Today, we are surprised at the depth of their medical knowledge. Of course, they did not use the same terms we use, and they lacked the technological understanding that we have, but manuals have been found that describe the importance of the heart and how it "speaks out" from the hands and the head (they were talking about the pulse). Doctors often worked with magicians to counteract snakebites and scorpion stings. Commoners wore amulets—special necklaces—to help bring down fevers, cure childhood ailments, and help with the dangers of childbirth. Mothers often hung necklaces that looked like fish

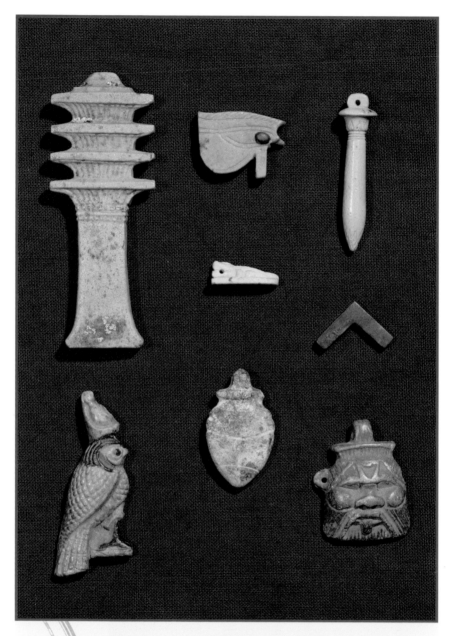

Although the Ancient Egyptians were skilled in medicine and science, they also liked to combine these subjects with their beliefs in magic. At a young age, people began wearing amulets *(above)* to ward off snakebites, scorpion stings, and sickness. Even mummies would have these pendants in their belongings for when they were reborn in the afterlife.

around their children's necks. It was thought that this symbol would protect them from falling in the river and drowning or being eaten by crocodiles. Garlic, lotus blossoms, juniper berries, and henna all played roles in medicine and magic. The instruments and medicines were quite crude, however, and people did not live very long lives.

HOMES

Wood was scarce, so the majority of homes were built from bricks made of mud from the Nile. The mud was collected in leather buckets, strengthened with straw and small pebbles, and poured into small, wooden frames. After the bricks dried in the sun, they were formed into walls and covered with limestone plaster. These adobe homes were relatively cool inside—even in the hotter months—because the windows were small, and the plaster acted as an insulator to keep out the heat. Mats covered the windows and doors, keeping insects and dust to a minimum

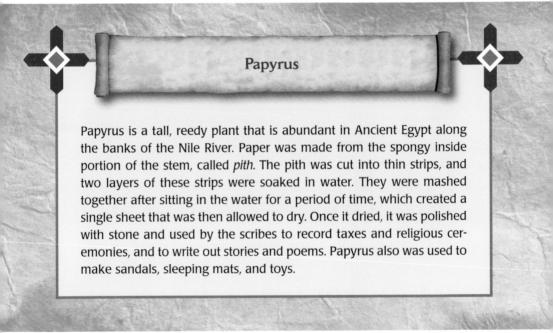

Papyrus

Papyrus is a tall, reedy plant that is abundant in Ancient Egypt along the banks of the Nile River. Paper was made from the spongy inside portion of the stem, called *pith*. The pith was cut into thin strips, and two layers of these strips were soaked in water. They were mashed together after sitting in the water for a period of time, which created a single sheet that was then allowed to dry. Once it dried, it was polished with stone and used by the scribes to record taxes and religious ceremonies, and to write out stories and poems. Papyrus also was used to make sandals, sleeping mats, and toys.

inside. Families often would paint elaborate decorative pictures of nature or scenes from everyday life on their walls. Floors were dirt and covered with papyrus mats, and ceilings were made of reeds or palm fronds woven together.

Homes of the commoners were constructed similarly to today's apartment buildings, but with open-air kitchens in courtyards that may have been shared by several families. These apartment-like homes had roof terraces on which children could play or families could sleep when it was very hot. The poor generally slept on reed mats on the floor.

The rich had large homes that included separate kitchens, bedrooms, and private apartments. Their walls enclosed gardens with flowering trees, sycamore figs, and date palms, as well as pools stocked with fish. Their ceilings were high and were supported by carved, stone columns. They had separate buildings for storing grain, stabling animals, and housing servants. The rich sometimes even had a separate small room (similar to a shower) in which a servant could pour water over them; the water would then drain out through holes in the tiled floor. They often slept on beds with simple mattresses of woven palms, covered with fine linens and animal skins. The inside walls of the home—rich or poor—had small niches in which the people would place statues of their favorite gods and goddesses; these were meant to safeguard their homes and families.

DIET

The Ancient Egyptians made use of everything around them; they took advantage of the Nile's flooding and the fertile soil left behind to grow all types of crops, including onions, garlic, leeks, beans, lentils, and lettuce. Barley and emmer wheat were used to bake bread, which was tough and contained grit from the grinding. This bread either was baked in a flat loaf, similar to a thick tortilla, or was formed into a longer, round loaf. Mummy teeth often show wear from chewing on this bread, which was a dietary staple for all classes. The Egyptians also used the barley and wheat to brew beer. Gourds, dates, figs, cucumbers, and melons were grown. Grapes were used for wine or dried into raisins. The poor ate little meat and poultry, but a large amount of fish, which was plentiful. Coarse linen spun from flax—a reed-like plant grown along the river—was used to weave nets with which the men would catch a variety of fish from the Nile that were boiled or dried in the sun to eat later. Duck, geese, oxen, pigs, sheep, and goats were slaughtered for banquets. A typical meal consisted of bread, vegetables and fruit, and beer. Wine and meat were eaten more often on special occasions.

SPECIAL OCCASIONS

Although the Egyptians worked hard, they also enjoyed having a good time. Scenes that depict festivals are everywhere—in tombs and on pottery, paintings, and hieroglyphics. Drawings and paintings of people dancing while musicians played flutes, harps, castanets, rhythm sticks, harps, string, and wind and percussion instruments are common. Of course, we have no way of knowing what the music sounded like, but—judging from the images—it seems that the music was loud and rousing. Most of these festivals were celebrations to honor the gods and included feasts and parades. Aside from these special events, men and women enjoyed swimming and boating on the Nile, as well as playing games. One contest pitted two men in boats against each other, with each trying to knock the other one into the water using a long stick. Noblemen often went hunting in the desert for rabbits, foxes, and larger animals such as gazelles.

CLOTHING, BEAUTY, AND FASHION

The Ancient Egyptians loved beauty and fashion. Both men and women used makeup, including paint for their eyes. Eye shadows of green, purple, and blue were made from natural elements ground into a fine powder and rubbed on the eyelids. Green eye paint symbolized fertility. A lead ore known as *galena* produced a gray-black paint we call *kohl* today. The Egyptians outlined their eyes with kohl, which created dramatic effects. Cheeks and lips were painted red using iron oxide, which was plentiful throughout the country. Some animal fat probably was mixed with the powders to help them adhere to the skin. Men and women alike used elaborate and beautiful containers to hold their makeup and creams, ointments, and perfumes.

Egyptians wore wigs of human hair and beeswax, but usually just for special occasions, and adorned their hair with garlands of flowers and combs. Young girls wore ponytails or pigtails, and boys' heads were usually shaved, with a braid hanging down one side. Plenty of paintings show Egyptians primping—using tweezers, curling their hair, shaving, and putting their hair up.

Everyone wore jewelry. Pierced earrings, necklaces, bracelets, and anklets were common, and the rich also wore special collars made of glass or pottery beads, jewels, gold, and silver. Nefertiti's famous bust shows her wearing nefer beads—long, gold beads—strung together into an elaborate necklace. Sandals were made of reed and papyrus or leather, and linen clothing was spun from flax (a plant fiber). The lower classes wore tunics of the same type of linen but more coarsely woven. The clothing of the rich was softer and the weave finer, or closer together. Depending on the season, men wore kilts (skirts) and women wore short dresses. Clothing was often pleated in fine, crisp folds. We do not know for sure how these pleats were achieved; however, grooved boards have been found, and it is thought that damp clothing was pressed into the grooves and then allowed to dry, creating the pleats. Young children did not bother with clothes in the warm weather, but their clothes were miniature versions of their parents in the winter.

THE MOST VALUABLE PROFESSION

The Ancient Egyptians invented paper and created one of the earliest forms of writing—in which they combined pictures and words—that became known as hieroglyphics. These word pictures are among the oldest writing in the world. Highly trained men called scribes (remember that women were not allowed to become scribes) kept all official written records for the country. To be a scribe was to be a highly regarded member of society. Scribes lived in the palace and ate the best foods, and they were exempt from paying taxes and from helping build pyramids, tombs, and temples. They began their training as young boys and worked hard at their trade; the training began at about age five and could take as long as twelve years. Scribes kept all of the government's records, including the amount of cattle in the royal herd and grain in the royal granaries. They also knew who owed taxes, and they recorded the height of the Nile's floodwaters and the success or failure of the year's grain crop. Common people turned to the scribes to write their wills or record their marriage contracts. Scribes also were highly trained in mathematics so they could keep accurate records of all the financial transactions of the land.

A large part of a scribe's responsibility was religious in nature. He wrote about the deeds performed by a person in his life, both good and bad. These records were kept on papyrus scrolls and buried with the dead; they were so prevalent in tombs of Ancient Egyptians that they became known as the "books of the dead." Scribes also kept track of supplies used to build a new temple and of the amounts and types of offerings made to the god or goddess. They kept long inventories of gifts made to the dead person for his journey to the afterlife.

Scribes often wrote for the upper class. They inscribed tombs, pottery, and limestone with the owners' names and details of their lives. They wrote about daily life, such as what kinds of tools craftsmen used, what kind of fish were caught in the Nile, how the women prepared the meals, and details of religious celebrations. Much of what we know about Ancient Egypt has been found on broken pieces of pottery called *ostraca,* preserved by the hot, dry climate and burial in sand.

Festivals were often a source of entertainment and relaxation for Ancient Egyptians. These events were documented with hieroglyphics depicting processions of warriors *(above)* and musicians, while others showed sumptuous feasts and sporting competitions.

Some scribes became famous; one—named Horemheb—even became a military general and later ruled as king. Another reason scribes were valued so highly by kings is because the kings realized that generations to come would know of them and their great (or not-so-great) works through the writings of the scribes; as a result, they treated the scribes with respect. Scribes not only were responsible for keeping records of crops, livestock, and other belongings, they recorded all legal proceedings and maintained legal documents. The upper class liked to read for pleasure, so scribes also were trained to write poetry, proverbs, and stories that were passed down through the generations.

It was difficult to learn to write the hieroglyphs used during this time. Hieroglyphs were elaborate symbols—more like writing with pictures than with words. There were more than 700 symbols in all, and they meant different things when used in different combinations. To make it even harder to learn and to decipher, hieroglyphs could be written in any direction. A fast form of hieroglyphs called *hieratic* was written from right to left, and an even faster version was used mainly for legal documents; this type of hieroglyphic "shorthand" was called *demotic*. Scribes were never without their traveling desk and supplies of papyrus, writing implements, and ink. Many paintings show scribes sitting cross-legged—hard at work—balancing a writing desk on their knees. Charcoal, red ocher, and blue and green minerals were ground up and used as ink. The scribe would spread the ink on a wooden palette, similar to a painter's palette, and would then dip in a writing instrument (something like a fine brush) with which to create the symbols.

We can thank the scribes and their devotion to keeping accurate and complete records for much of what we have learned about the lives and times of the Ancient Egyptians.

4

Religion

LIFE WAS SHORT AND DIFFICULT FOR THE ANCIENT EGYPTIANS. ABOUT HALF of all children died by the time they were 10, and half of all adults died by their fortieth birthday. Their lives were made easier, however, by their reliance on hundreds of different gods for everything from an abundant harvest to healthy children. Their *polytheistic* (belief in more than one god) religion was at the center of their daily lives, and they found comfort in the belief that there were beings greater than themselves to whom they could entrust their every need. As part of their religious beliefs, the gods were the "owners" of the universe, and anything good that happened was attributed to them. If a battle was won, the weather was good, the crops were plentiful, or water was found in the desert, it meant that the gods were pleased. Conversely, if bad things happened—a drought, plague, or poor harvest—the people must have done something to draw the gods' wrath, and sacrifices and offerings were required to make the gods happy again. One common sacrifice was the killing of a calf, which might be draped with garlands of flowers before it was slaughtered.

LIFE AFTER DEATH

At the core of their religion was the belief in an afterlife. The Ancient Egyptians believed that, if they lived good lives on Earth, they would be rewarded with going to a special land after they died. To them, death was only a transition from life on Earth to a better life afterward. They believed the afterlife was a place similar to Egypt—that it contained all the beauty of their beloved land—but that it had none of the hardships they also lived with.

Life after death was not all rosy, however. There was an underworld called the *Duat*, part of which was filled with dangerous snakes and fire, or men waiting to attack you. Spells to avoid these dangers were written in hieroglyphics on coffins. Eventually the spells were written on scrolls of paper made from the papyrus plant. These scrolls, often referred to as "books of the dead," were found buried with mummies. They might be individualized for a specific person, but all included information and advice to help the newly dead person navigate the dangers of the underworld, in part by explaining how to recite the spells at just the right time. One interesting belief about the underworld was found within the Hall of the Two Truths, in which the deceased's heart was weighed against his or her past deeds. If a person had done wicked things during his life, his past deeds would weigh more than his heart, and he would fail the test—meaning that terrible things waited for him. If he had a light heart that was free from evil, he was headed for a

Like other religions of the world, the Egyptians believed a person had to earn a happy afterlife. As depicted in this version of the Book of the Dead, when a person died, they would face the god Anubis, who judged each person by weighing the person's heart against his or her misdeed. Depending on which was heavier, Anubis would send the person to either a land of relaxation and happiness or a place of pain and terror.

wonderful afterlife in a land just like Egypt, but without all the hard work and difficulties.

As with all religions, the Egyptians had creation stories that explained how life began. Most of the tales explain that, in the beginning of time, nothing existed except the "Waters of Chaos." Some stories say that a lotus flower opened its petals to reveal the sun god as a baby. Others say that a bit of dry land appeared and a large bird flew to it, landed, and laid an egg that became the world. Still another story says that a god lived in the Waters of Chaos for many years. Eventually he realized that he was lonely, so he created other gods and goddesses and then a world—with Egypt and her people at the center. These gods usually took the forms of animals, or were part animal and part human. They often wore elaborate headdresses and carried staffs or other objects. Often these objects bore the symbol of life, the ankh. One of the most important gods was Amun-Ra, the king of the gods—the sun god and ruler of the universe—because without him, there would be no life on Earth. Osiris, the god of the underworld, was equally important; without him, there would be no life after death.

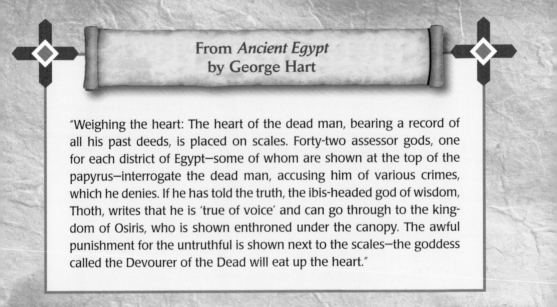

From *Ancient Egypt*
by George Hart

"Weighing the heart: The heart of the dead man, bearing a record of all his past deeds, is placed on scales. Forty-two assessor gods, one for each district of Egypt—some of whom are shown at the top of the papyrus—interrogate the dead man, accusing him of various crimes, which he denies. If he has told the truth, the ibis-headed god of wisdom, Thoth, writes that he is 'true of voice' and can go through to the kingdom of Osiris, who is shown enthroned under the canopy. The awful punishment for the untruthful is shown next to the scales—the goddess called the Devourer of the Dead will eat up the heart."

MUMMIFICATION

Thanks to the hot, dry climate, bodies were naturally preserved after they were buried and surrounded by sand, which would draw all the moisture from the body, dehydrating it. Once the Egyptians began burying their dead in coffins to protect the bodies from animals, they realized that the bodies would decompose rapidly if not allowed to dehydrate—the moisture in the ground causes bodies to deteriorate and decay. Gradually, they developed elaborate methods to embalm the body, which preserved many of them for centuries. According to Milton Meltzer, author of *In the Days of the Pharaohs*, Persians saw some bodies being embalmed and thought that the dark coating or the resin on the outside was bitumen (a material made from tar or petroleum). Their word for this coating was *mummia* (the word *mumma* meant "preserved bodies"), and eventually the bodies inside the linen coverings became known as mummies.

Because the Egyptians believed the body would return to its former state after death, it was important to them to preserve it in as lifelike a manner as possible so the dead would be whole again in the afterlife. Over the years, they developed an intricate process of drying the body that was so effective that—more than 3,000 years later—we can get an accurate picture of what the dead person looked like. This process is called embalming, and ended with the body looking like the mummies we are familiar with today.

By the time of the eighteenth dynasty, when Nefertiti ruled, Egyptians had perfected mummification to an art form, leaving us with some of the best examples of mummies from the ancient era—including King Tut's mummy and the mummy some scholars think is Nefertiti. Priests were in charge of the mummification process. They were the only ones who knew the proper prayers to say, and they had the necessary knowledge of the human body. The mummification process took more than two months—70 days, to be exact—and was quite involved. All of the internal organs had to be removed and the body dried. The first organ to come out was the brain, which was removed by long hooks that pulled out brain tissue through the nose. All of the internal organs were then removed through an incision in the stomach—except for the heart, which was left in place because the Egyptians believed that the heart was the center of a person's intelligence and soul. The other organs were specially treated and sometimes placed in containers of wood, pottery, limestone, or bronze called canopic jars that went in the burial chamber with the mummy. Sometimes the organs were wrapped individually and replaced in the body.

The body was then coated with a special salt called natron and left to dry. When it was completely dried out, the natron was wiped off and the body looked like a raisin, wrinkled and sunken. The areas that were quite shriveled would sometimes be stuffed with wads of linen to fill them out. False eyes were sometimes placed in the eye sockets. The empty shell of the body then was treated with oils and perfumes, and wrapped in many yards of torn strips of linen. Great care was taken to cover every part of the body separately and completely to protect it. Sometimes fingers and toes were individually wrapped. The whole time a body was being wrapped, priests said prayers and placed amulets and special items within the wrappings to ward off evil. Depending on the status of the deceased, the body might then be placed in several coffins and finally laid to rest in a large tomb of stone. The Egyptians believed that the soul that survived in the afterlife would eventually be reunited with its body, but it needed to be able to recognize it to become whole again, which is why they took such care to preserve the body.

Not only was the mummified body placed in the tomb, but—depending on the wealth of the individual—many personal belongs would be buried as well. These items included furniture, clothing, food, jewelry, paintings, and so on: anything that would make the deceased's existence in the afterlife more comfortable. Finally, during the actual burial, the priest would touch a special instrument to each of the body's parts to help it live well in the afterlife. This would include the eyes, so the deceased could see, and the mouth, so he could speak. Burial rituals could be quite elaborate. The very rich would hire professional mourners, who would cry and moan and throw sand in the air during the funeral. The more mourners there were, the greater the power or rank of the dead man.

Pharoahs and members of the royal family were always mummified, as were most members of the upper class. Commoners were not preserved in this way as often, because it was an expensive and time-consuming process. Interestingly, many animals also were mummified. Pet cats were the most common animal to be preserved, and they often had miniature faces painted on the linen that covered their faces. Crocodiles and birds, which were significant to some gods, also were sometimes mummified. Pets might be mummified after they died a natural death—and then buried with their master—but sometimes they

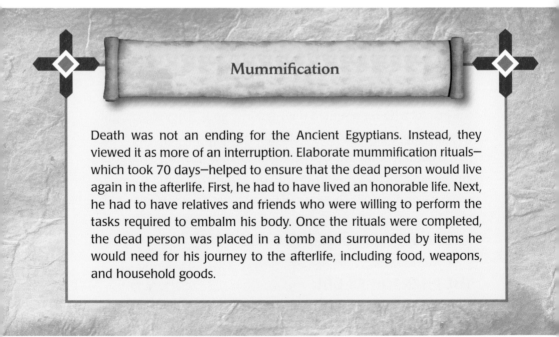

Mummification

Death was not an ending for the Ancient Egyptians. Instead, they viewed it as more of an interruption. Elaborate mummification rituals—which took 70 days—helped to ensure that the dead person would live again in the afterlife. First, he had to have lived an honorable life. Next, he had to have relatives and friends who were willing to perform the tasks required to embalm his body. Once the rituals were completed, the dead person was placed in a tomb and surrounded by items he would need for his journey to the afterlife, including food, weapons, and household goods.

were killed at the time their master died, in order to be placed within the coffin.

TEMPLES

Temples were built to honor each god; even the minor deities had a place for the people to come and worship. Inside the temple, which was usually carved of stone, a sanctuary was accessible to the public. Within that common area, a shrine was built that only the priests were allowed to enter. Although each temple was different, the basic elements were the same. Surrounded by a high wall with a courtyard, complete with other small buildings that served as homes for the priests, warehouses, and offices, every temple was like a home for its god. The chief priest of the temple was kept busy bringing food and other offerings to the sculpture that resembled the god or goddess. The priest also would dress the statue in garlands of flowers and put perfume on it, in an effort to keep the god happy. The stone image of the god was brought out of the shrine only for special occasions, when the common people would come to celebrate and pay homage.

The people believed that caring for the god in this way would keep it happy—and if the gods were happy, Egypt and her people would be kept safe and prosperous. Kings gave money to the priests who represented their favorite gods. They also might give food, goods, and slaves to the priest to help with the upkeep of the temple. Sometimes people came to pay tribute to the god, and encampments grew up around the temple, luring craftsmen, teachers, and artists. These small towns—each with its own god, temple, and religious organization—were centers of religious life as well as economic and intellectual activity.

THE PHARAOH AS GOD

Although the pharaoh was believed to be a god, he did not become a deity until he was crowned and actually took over

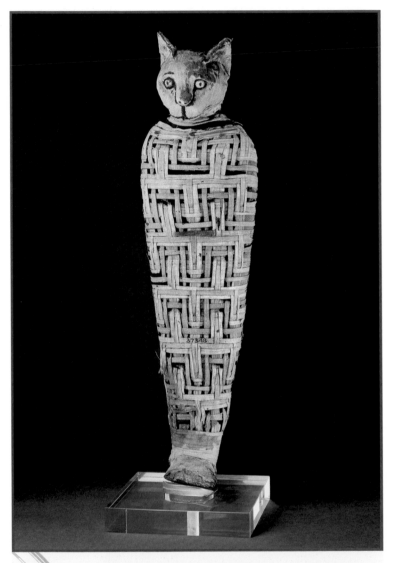

Cats were so revered in Ancient Egypt, rich families often mummified their felines when they died, or killed the pet for mummification if the owner passed away before the cat *(above)*. This obsession with cats was based on the Ancient Egyptians' devotion to Bastet, the cat goddess of joy, music, and dancing. Love for cats was said to be so fierce, the Greek historian Herodotus witnessed an Egyptian family shaving their eyebrows in mourning when their family cat died.

the position of pharaoh. Then he became the link between the physical world and the afterlife and was considered the high priest to all the gods. The priests were the intermediaries between the world of men and the gods; the high priest held the most power and was responsible for the temple treasures and land. This position was often passed down from father to son for generations. Lower-level priests served at individual temples by keeping the records and maintaining temple property. Women sometimes were allowed to serve in the temples by assisting the priests with minor tasks and rituals. The priest also was something of an official astronomer, recording where different stars were located and how they were grouped.

In addition to the political power she may have wielded, it is believed that Nefertiti also served as a priestess to the sun-disk god, Aten. Some images survive that show Nefertiti performing religious rituals along with her husband, the Pharaoh Akhenaten. In one famous relief, she is shown standing with Akhenaten and two of their daughters, holding up offerings to Aten.

GODS AND GODDESSES

The sun god, Amun-Ra, was the dominant deity responsible for all life, and the most powerful of the gods. He sometimes was depicted as a man with the head of a ram, and at other times as a man wearing a headdress with two plumes in it. His temple at Karnak, outside of Luxor, is one of the largest and most complex in the country.

Another popular god was Thoth—the god of the moon—who was represented by the ibis, a type of bird. Thoth was the patron of the scribes and was believed to have given humans the knowledge of writing, medicine, and math. The goddess Bastet was the daughter of Ra. Represented as a woman with the head of a cat, she used the power of the sun to ripen crops. Osiris was the god of the underworld, usually portrayed as a green-skinned man dressed like a pharaoh. He was the son of Ra, and he decided whether or not to allow the newly dead to enter the afterlife. Anubis—depicted as a man with the head of a dog—was the god of embalming and mummification, as well as the god of the underworld before Osiris. Another popular god was Bes, the god of music and dance. He also served as the protector of the family and watched out for children by protecting them against evil spirits. He was portrayed as part dwarf, part lion, and he carried a sword to ward off danger. Horus, a very early god, had the head of a hawk and the body of a man. He was the protector of the pharaoh and god of the sky.

Many animals held special significance to the Ancient Egyptians. Although they were not worshiped in their own right, these animals—including scarab beetles, crocodiles, bulls, falcons, the ibis, and the cat—were considered sacred. The people believed that different gods and goddesses cared about these animals; to show reverence to the deity, it was only proper to treat the animal in a special way. Each town, in addition to having its own god, had a sacred animal that was kept at the temple and cared for carefully. Sacred trees also were identified. Sycamores were apparently quite popular, as they are often depicted in paintings and drawings. Egypt comprised 42 *nomes*, or administrative districts, which were similar to states. In addition to the main gods and those for each town, each nome had its own gods. Sometimes the same animal was used to represent different gods in the different nomes. As you can imagine, this could get pretty confusing.

A person's name was all-important to the Ancient Egyptians. Just like today, a person's name provided his or her identity. The Egyptians believed that you could destroy a person's soul by erasing his or her name—whether on the tomb or in a business document, letter, or poem. Conversely, if you spoke someone's name out loud at a certain time after he or she died, you could help him or her advance to a better place in the afterlife. The fact that Nefertiti's name was erased or destroyed on many ancient writings and reliefs is proof to some Egyptologists that she had many enemies who wanted to do the ultimate damage to her.

The rules surrounding worship seem very complicated to us today. However, the basic religious beliefs were simply a normal part of life in Ancient Egypt.

5

Egyptian Royalty

NOT ONLY WAS THE PHARAOH, OR KING, THE ULTIMATE RULER OF THE country, but once he was crowned, he also was considered a god. The word *pharaoh* means "great house" and originally referred to the large palace in which the king lived with his wife, children, and courtiers—people who lived and worked in the palace. Eventually, around the time that Nefertiti lived, the word pharaoh also came to mean the ruler himself.

The pharaoh wielded absolute power over his subjects, but because the country was so large, he had to entrust much of that power to his officials, especially the priests. Each of the country's 42 regions, or nomes, was overseen by a special official. Each nome had its temples, and each temple had a priest; as a result, there were many layers of power below the king. Although most

of these officials were probably trustworthy, there were undoubt-
edly those who misused their power, ordering people around or
gaining special favors for their friends. In return for being loyal
assistants to the king, honest officials were rewarded by having
their tombs built near his. It was believed that they also would
be rewarded in the afterlife, earning eternal life in a wonderful
place for their upstanding behavior while alive.

The pharaoh had many duties to perform as part of his
job. One of them was to preserve *maat*, which was the Egyptian word for "order, truth, and justice." These three qualities
were very important to them and were symbolized by a goddess
named Ma'at, portrayed either as a woman holding an ostrich
feather or as just a feather. The Ancient Egyptians were a very
orderly people. They believed that the universe was a moral and
harmonious place, and they relied on the king to establish and
maintain that order and balance. There were no gray areas in
the peoples' behaviors. You were either good and rewarded, or
you were bad and punished.

As part of his duties, the king also was supposed to visit
each part of the country at least once every two years to ensure
that the temples were being cared for and that the officials
of each nome were performing their jobs honestly, as well
as to check on the general welfare of his country. This meant
that the king (and his family) moved around a lot, so several
palaces—in addition to the main one, located in the capital city
where he spent most of his time—were built in various parts
of the country. The king's job might sound simple, but again,
because of the sheer size of the country and the number of its
people, it was not always an easy job to accomplish. Getting
around was difficult, too. There were no trains or highways to
whisk him from place to place. Generally, people traveled by
foot, although camels and donkeys were ridden later. The very
rich (or royals) might have slaves carry them in special chairs
known as *litters*. Chariots and horses did not come along until
much later.

As we have already seen, festivals and celebrations played a big part in the lives of the Egyptian people. After a king had reigned for 30 years, a large celebration was held to renew his powers and strengthen the balance of his life as king. He appealed to the gods to keep him strong and wise, to continue to uphold *maat*, and to continue to provide well for his people. Or, if harvests had been poor and people had been suffering, he would appeal to the gods to turn the bad fortune around and make everything good again.

ROYAL BURIALS

Life after death was a powerful belief of the Ancient Egyptians, and they spent their lives preparing for it. Most of the kings prepared by having temples and elaborate tombs built while they were still alive. Many of these burial chambers were so intricate and large, they took years to build and decorate with wall paintings and sculptures. The most well-known tombs, of course, are the pyramids in Giza, especially what is known as the Great Pyramid. This magnificent structure was built as the burying place for the Pharaoh Khufu in about 2540 B.C. Probably the best-known tomb is the one that belongs to King Tutenkhaman, or King Tut. The "boy king," as he is commonly known, had one of the only tombs that was found virtually undisturbed. The bounty found there verifies the myths of the ancient pharaoh's great wealth and treasures.

The pharaoh wore special clothing, and each item had a special meaning. The crown he wore was actually a double crown—one part was tall and white to symbolize Upper Egypt, and another part was flatter and red for Lower Egypt. It was believed that when the king wore a bull's tail on his kilt, or skirt, he had the strength of a bull. Because Egyptian men were clean-shaven, the king needed to differentiate himself as a living god, so he would wear a false beard in public. This false beard possibly was made of human hair and looked something like a long

The discovery of King Tutenkhamen's burial chamber and tomb *(above)* was one of the greatest archaeological finds in Egypt. Uncovered in 1922, King Tut's tomb was an exceptionally lucky find because it was one of the few graves from its time period that was intact and untouched by robbers.

goatee—but wider at the bottom—and was held in place by thin wires looped over the ears. The king also carried a scepter—a long rod or staff that symbolized his authority, especially over his enemies. Paintings show pharaohs holding their scepters overhead while a cringing captive lies on the ground, waiting to be hit.

The royals were distinguished by their finely woven linen clothing, headdresses of gold and jewels, and elaborate jewelry and makeup. The headdress on the bust of Queen Nefertiti, for example, is distinctive: a tall, barrel-shaped crown of bright blue with bands of gold and red. In many paintings of kings and queens, they can be seen wearing headdresses with cobras on them. Only members of the royal family were allowed to wear the cobra goddess, for the goddess Wadjet, who was believed to protect them by spitting flames at their enemies. Sometimes they wore the images of two gods, Wadjet (of Lower Egypt) and Nekhbet, the vulture goddess of Upper Egypt; both were protectors of women and children. These two symbols signified that, although Egypt was one country, it still comprised two regions with distinct personalities. Together, the two goddesses were known as the "two ladies of the pharaoh."

The pharaoh's first, or primary, wife was considered a goddess and was called the "Great Royal Wife." If she had a son, he would become the next king. If she had only daughters, as in the case of Nefertiti, one of the secondary wives' sons would be next in line for the throne. It was in the best interests of the country to pass power from father to son as seamlessly as possible, so grooming of the young prince was begun early, to prepare him to lead his people. Training for the kingship included an excellent education and military training. Quite often, the prince had to rule at a very young age because of the death of his father. When this happened, he ruled with a co-regent—a trusted member of the royal court or family who acted as a coruler—until he was old enough to rule on his own. Very often, the co-regent was the prince's mother or one of the king's lesser wives. In some cases, the co-regent liked his or her power so much, the prince was pushed out of position and the co-regent took over as king. It was also common for kings to marry their sister or another close relation, a habit that was not practiced by commoners.

WHAT ABOUT THE WOMEN?

Women generally did not hold positions of power in Ancient Egypt, but the king's mother always was considered important and was revered. This was true for Akhenaten's mother, Queen Tiye, who was known as a wise older woman. By all accounts, she was a powerful woman and quite influential at court.

In some rituals and festivals, the king's female relatives might play the parts of goddesses. If the crown prince was too young to rule on his own when his father, the king, died, often one of the king's female relatives would serve as a co-regent. His mother or wife might be chosen, or they volunteered to serve in this position. Some of these women became well known in their own right. Nefertiti may have served as co-regent to Tutenkhamen, who was only nine when he ascended to the throne.

Women rulers were rare but not unknown. Nitocris was possibly the first female pharaoh, reigning as the last pharaoh of the sixth dynasty, after the death of Pepy II. About 400 years later, Sobeknefru, who had been co-regent with her father, ruled for three years during the Middle Kingdom—she is the first confirmed female pharaoh. Queen Ahhotep ruled for her son, Ahmose, and led troops into battle. Queen Tiye, the wife of Amenhotep III, was not born into a royal family, but she was a highly respected and influential woman, as already mentioned. Tiye was from Nubia; she was the daughter of an official in the court of Amenhotep II, who would become her father-in-law. She supposedly married at age 11 or 12 and was recognized as quite intelligent. Some Egyptologists believe that her son, Amenhotep IV—who later changed his name to Akhenaten— was heavily influenced in his radical religious and cultural beliefs by his mother and her foreign background.

One of the most famous female rulers was Hatshepsut, who ruled for 20 years and has become known as the "female pharaoh." She was the daughter of Thutmose II; when he died, his son (Thutmose III) by a lesser wife became king, and Hatshepsut took over as co-regent. She eventually pushed her stepson out of the way and ruled on her own—she even wore the pharaoh's crown. Despite what some considered her "pushy" ways, she was regarded as a good leader, excellent at foreign policy,

Nefertiti, while beautiful and intelligent, was unable to produce sons for her pharaoh. Because Egyptian tradition dictates the pharaoh's power must transfer from father to son, the offspring of a lesser wife was chosen to rule Egypt. The unfinished head of Queen Nefertiti *(above)*, created from brown quartzite, dates from the Amarna period.

and responsible for the building of many monuments. At some point, she must have decided that she would demand more respect as a man—she changed her title from queen to king and was shown wearing men's clothing and a false beard. She died in 1483 B.C., leaving her stepson to rule for another 20 years. Perhaps the most famous female ruler, however, was Cleopatra VII, who ruled about 1400 years later. History tells us she was intelligent, ambitious, charming, and politically skillful.

Some young men served for decades. Pharaoh Pepy II may hold the record for the longest rule—some believe that he served for 94 years as the last king of the sixth dynasty, at the end of the First Intermediate period. (Some Egyptologists believe instead that he reigned for 64 years.) He was just 6 years old when he came to the throne, which would have made him 100 when he died. Tuthmosis IV reigned during the eighteenth dynasty and became famous for uncovering the Sphinx from the sand, based on what he was told in a dream. One of the most famous of the Egyptian pharaohs was Ramses II of the nineteenth dynasty. He took the throne when he was approximately 20 years old and reigned for 66 years. He was known for being a powerful ruler and for having more than 100 children by many wives. Although we know each of these kings by one (or perhaps two) names, most of them had five names in all. Their birth name was the family name, and they took a throne name when they were crowned. These names were written inside an oval called a cartouche, which symbolized the sun—the giver of all life. The cartouche for any individual king or queen could be found on their headdresses, in paintings and sculptures that told about their lives, and, of course, on their tombs.

KING TUT

Today, most people recognize the name of Tutenkhamen—or King Tut, for short. He also is known as the "Boy King," because he took the throne while still a young boy of about nine years old and died before his twentieth birthday. Nefertiti was his mother-in-law as well as his stepmother. (Tut married one of the daughters of Nefertiti and Akhenaten, and he was the son of

Akhenaten and Kiya, one of Akhenaten's secondary wives.)

We know more about Tut today because of the discovery of his tomb in 1922 than for anything he accomplished as pharaoh. His burial chamber was found virtually intact—the only royal tomb to remain so undisturbed. Because some items were in disarray, Egyptologists believe ancient tomb raiders tried to rob it, but they must have been interrupted by guards before they could do serious damage. The treasures found in Tut's tomb included many items of gold and fine jewels, in addition to the standard everyday items required in the afterlife, such as furniture and toiletries. Tut's tomb was relatively small for a king; it had only four small rooms, and the space was crammed with his possessions. It is theorized that a more sizeable tomb was being built, but that it was unfinished at the time of his death. The bright gold mask that covered the face of his mummy has become famous around the world and symbolizes the richness and grandeur of Ancient Egypt.

6

The Lost City of Amarna and King Tut's Tomb

THE HISTORY OF THE CITY OF AMARNA IS BARELY A BLIP ON THE TIMELINE of the thousands of years of Egyptian history. Although it lasted only about 30 years, the Amarna period stands out as a distinct era in Ancient Egypt. Amarna was located on the eastern banks of the Nile River, approximately midway between Thebes to the south and Memphis to the north—both former capital cities. Most Egyptologists agree that Amarna was a new city, built to the specifications of Akhenaten and Nefertiti to provide a secluded place in which to worship Aten, the sun-disk god. The pharaoh originally named the city Akhenaten—which meant "The Aten has come"—and then took the same name for himself. Today the site is known as El-Amarna, or, more simply, Amarna.

Akhenaten and Nefertiti brought with them many people—between 10,000 and 20,000—to populate the city, which they saw as a haven. It may have been the retreat they desired, and the religion may have flourished, but only for a time. The country was in need of a strong ruler, one who could pay attention to foreign and economic affairs. Instead, what they seemed to get was one somewhat out of touch with reality—a dreamer—who ultimately may have let his country down.

NEFERTITI'S HUSBAND

Akhenaten was crowned king in 1352 B.C. in Thebes, the center of religion and culture that was devoted to Amun-Ra, god of the sun and all life. Thebes was a busy city, and it teemed with those who earned their living by serving Amun-Ra. Religion was the big business of the day and supported thousands of ancillary workers, including not only the high priest and lesser priests but also all of the administrative workers in the temples and those who took care of them (farmers, woodworkers, their families, and so on).

Thebes was not the only bustling city. Up and down the Nile, temples were built to honor the gods who had blessed Egypt with many years of prosperity and security, and towns grew up around these centers of religion, commerce, and culture. The thriving religion business benefited the many priests and other temple workers; with each new temple and city that was built, the power of the priests grew. They had great influence—not only over religion but also over politics and culture. Some believe that Akhenaten's move to monotheism was made purely to thwart some of that power. Although this did curb the priests' power somewhat, they still managed to influence people, judging by the remains found.

Akhenaten was the second son of the Pharoah Amenhotep III and Queen Tiye, who was not Egyptian but came from

Nubia, and married Amenhotep when she was only about 12 years old. Later images of Queen Tiye portray a strong older woman who carried herself gracefully. She became known as the "wise woman" in Nefertiti's court, and she was likely a great influence on her daughter-in-law. As Akhenaten became increasingly involved in religious matters, it seems he relied on two relatives to run the military and diplomatic parts of his government. His father-in-law, Ay, and his brother-in-law, General Horemheb (married to Nefertiti's sister) kept order for Akhenaten. Each of these two would serve Egypt as pharaoh after the death of King Tutenkhamen.

Akhenaten's older brother, Tuthmose, who should have become king on the death of their father, died suddenly near the end of Amenhotep's reign. So Akhenaten—although he was not even 20 years old at the time—became pharaoh in 1370 B.C., supported by his mother. Akhenaten's real name was Amenhotep IV, and he used that name as king. Just a few years later, however—after he decided to revise the country's religion—he took the name Akhenaten in honor of the god Aten. Some believe that Akhenaten was more or less ignored as a child, excluded from family activities (he had four sisters and one brother) and unblessed by the god Amun-Ra. Images made during his childhood often do not include him, but Queen Tiye seems to have had a soft spot in her heart for him. Some feel that the queen's childhood religion was much simpler than that of her husband, and that she impressed different beliefs on her son, encouraging his monotheism.

In the portraits and stone reliefs in which he does appear, Akhenaten is almost always depicted in a somewhat deformed way. Some scientists believe that the future king was born with a genetic deformity caused by a disease called Marfan syndrome, which damages the body's connective tissue. Those who have this disease have an elongated head and very long limbs, but a short body with a potbelly and little muscle tone.

After changing the religion of all of Egypt, Ahmenhotep IV revised his own name to Akhenaten. Images of this pharaoh are unique because he is depicted with a long, narrow face, exaggerated features, and a small potbelly. Unlike the pharaohs before him, who are all sculpted as the ideal man, some believe Akhenaten purposely portrayed himself differently because it was how he truly looked.

If this diagnosis is true, it would explain why his images look so odd.

Despite the natural boundaries surrounding the country that helped to protect it from foreign invaders—the Sahara, two seas, and the Nile (with its dangerous rapids and predators like the hippo and crocodile)—Egypt always needed to be on guard against those who wanted to infiltrate it. Unfortunately, Akhenaten was either unaware of the realities of these invaders or just could not focus on anything other than worshiping Aten. He ignored letters from military leaders to the east, in which they begged for his help. Perhaps he thought that earthly battles did not matter, and that only what happened after death was worthy of his attention. Maybe he was a pacifist, or maybe he felt that the Egyptian people deserved to be punished for their reluctance or refusal to accept his belief in Aten. Whatever

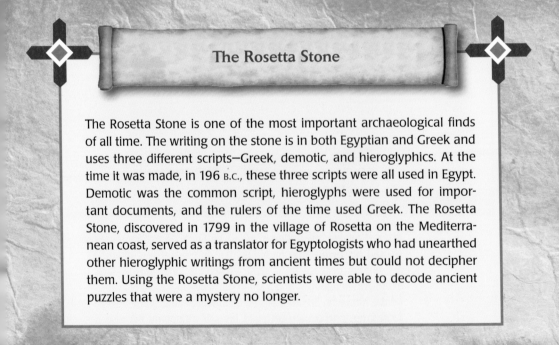

The Rosetta Stone

The Rosetta Stone is one of the most important archaeological finds of all time. The writing on the stone is in both Egyptian and Greek and uses three different scripts—Greek, demotic, and hieroglyphics. At the time it was made, in 196 B.C., these three scripts were all used in Egypt. Demotic was the common script, hieroglyphs were used for important documents, and the rulers of the time used Greek. The Rosetta Stone, discovered in 1799 in the village of Rosetta on the Mediterranean coast, served as a translator for Egyptologists who had unearthed other hieroglyphic writings from ancient times but could not decipher them. Using the Rosetta Stone, scientists were able to decode ancient puzzles that were a mystery no longer.

his reasons, gains made in foreign relations decades earlier by Thutmose III and his successors were lost during the Amarna period.

UNWELCOME CHANGES

During the royal couple's experimentation with religion, many Egyptians complied with the command to deny the other thousands of gods and honor only Aten; but artifacts from this period have been found throughout the country, and even in Amarna itself, that relate to the old gods. These archaeological finds are proof that Akhenaten's command to practice a mono-theistic religion never completely took hold in the country. Perhaps those who seemingly agreed with him actually worshiped as they wished in the privacy of their own homes, and only pretended to worship Aten to stay in the good graces of their king.

The sun-disk god, Aten, was not a new god; he had been worshiped as part of the sun god, Ra, during the Old Kingdom. Aten was the only god who did not take human or animal form—he was depicted as a sun with long rays that resembled arms. The rays ended in open hands, offering life and peace to all living things. The god Amun (or Amun-Ra) was pictured as a man wearing a tall hat with long plumes rising out of it. He was believed to be the king of all gods, existing before the creation of the world. Originally, Akhenaten had built a temple near Amun's at Karnak, the great complex of temples and shrines to Amun, near Thebes. The fact that Akhenaten had elevated Aten to the status of Amun-Ra was impossible for the people to accept. After all, Amun-Ra was the giver of all life, the king of the gods. He existed before the world had shape or form. Aten, in their eyes, might be a part of him, but he could never rise to the same level of importance. When Akhenaten decreed that Amun-Ra's temples should be closed and that he was no longer to be worshiped, the people rebelled.

Akhenaten is often called the "heretic king" today. Some scholars say that he had a vision of a disk of light sitting between two mountains. He believed that this vision told him to make a change: to pursue monotheism and to build a city dedicated to Aten in an area between two mountains. Through all these changes, Nefertiti was by his side, and some believe she actually pushed him to make the changes in the first place.

ARCHITECTURE IN AMARNA

When Amarna was designed, it included a large temple to Aten—which was built in a manner completely different from past temples—and a smaller temple. Because the sun disk was one dimensional, the rooms did not have to be large enough to accommodate three-dimensional sculptures of the god. Temples normally were closed, and they contained an outer room, an inner sanctuary, and a roof. Because Aten was seen as the sun that warmed the Earth and helped crops to grow, the temple was built without a roof so the sun's rays could penetrate the temple, lighting it and honoring Aten. This temple contained several courtyards, many altars, and painted scenes of Aten's rays holding the ankh. Around the temples were offices and homes for the priests and their helpers, and bakeries in which bread would be baked every day for offerings to Aten. Any leftovers were given to the priests and other temple employees.

Two palaces were built in Amarna: one in the northern part of the city and the other at the opposite, or southernmost, end. In between was a village for workers, as well as two other residential areas. The various parts of the city were connected by wide roads. Akhenaten also oversaw the building of the royal tomb. It was similar in design to other tombs found throughout Egypt, but it had additional rooms that included the remains of a granite sarcophagus. Archaeologists were able to reconstruct enough of this coffin to show images of Queen Nefertiti on the four corners, extending her arms as if to protect her husband in death. Egyptologists believe that Akhenaten's body was buried there originally, but his mummy has never been found.

His body may have been destroyed by enemies or hidden in an unmarked tomb by his loyal followers who wanted to protect it for the afterlife.

Amarna was deserted—and much of it was destroyed—but no other city was built on the ruins. The sand eventually covered it completely, helping to preserve its treasures, which offer much information about these rulers of the eighteenth dynasty and the way their people lived.

CHANGE IN ART

Egyptian artists generally portrayed their human subjects in formal, stylized ways, with the head, legs, and feet shown in profile, and the body shown from the front. Arms and sides were stiff, and facial expressions were dignified. Nefertiti and Akhenaten, however, encouraged artists to portray them in natural, affectionate, and playful poses, demonstrating a new realism that extended to other artwork as well. Statues became more full-figured and curvy. For example, Akhenaten and Nefertiti both are shown as having slight potbellies.

Most who write about art during the Amarna period mention the softly naturalistic style adopted by painters and sculptures. Although it is believed that Nefertiti lent a feminine, softening touch to the stark reality of the sun-disk Aten, just how much effect this had on the art world is unknown. Some critics call the style of this time caricature, because images of Akhenaten and his family were often misshapen and appeared as a joke. Whatever the intent of the artists of the Amarna period, they brought a new dimension to Egyptian art that influenced subsequent generations.

THE BOY KING

Of all the famous names from the era of the Ancient Egyptian pharaohs—Cleopatra, Ramses, Seti, Nefertiti, and so on—we perhaps feel as if we know one the best. For us, he has come to symbolize the entire scope of Ancient Egypt: the pomp, riches, royalty, and mystery. We know this symbol as King Tut, the boy king. Tut, or Tutenkhamen, ruled for only a few brief years; he came to the throne at about the age of 9 or 10, in about 1334 B.C., and died at age 19. He was born in Amarna to the Pharaoh Akhenaten and one of his secondary wives, Kiya. When he was about 12 years old, he married his half-sister, Ankhesenamun, who was the daughter of Pharaoh Akhenaten and Queen Nefertiti. This made Nefertiti not only his step-mother but also his mother-in-law.

Tut's original name was Tutankhaten, which means "living image of the Aten." At about the time that he married Ankhe-senamun, he moved the court back to the previous capital at Thebes, restored polytheistic religion, and changed his name to Tutenkhamen, which means "living image of the Amun." Tut's wife was approximately two or three years older than he was, and the couple is thought to have had two daughters, both of whom were stillborn. Scholars believe this to be the case because two tiny, mummified female babies were found within the burial chambers of King Tut.

Tut did not rule for very long, but he did make an impact on the country with his restoration of temples around the land, as well as the restoration of the old religious beliefs his father had tried to eradicate. The priests condemned Akhene-ten and ordered his name erased wherever possible, then they took advantage of Tut's reversal to regain the power they had lost. The boy king died from what most researchers agree was a head wound; whether it was an accident or he was murdered is not known. Because he died unexpectedly, construction on his tomb was not yet completed, and he was buried in a small tomb that may have been intended for someone else—probably a court official. The tomb consisted of four small rooms that were crowded with objects meant for him to use in the afterlife, including jewelry, instruments, furniture, cloth-ing, model boats, and weapons. As previously mentioned,

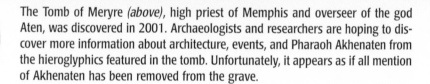

The Tomb of Meryre *(above)*, high priest of Memphis and overseer of the god Aten, was discovered in 2001. Archaeologists and researchers are hoping to discover more information about architecture, events, and Pharaoh Akhenaten from the hieroglyphics featured in the tomb. Unfortunately, it appears as if all mention of Akhenaten has been removed from the grave.

disarray within the rooms led many to believe that thieves tried to rob the burial chamber at some point but were interrupted in their attempts. The entrance was resealed and soon hidden under sand and debris from nearby tombs that were under construction.

After about 2150 B.C., most pharaohs were buried in the Valley of the Kings, outside Thebes's city limits. Guards often were posted at the entrances to the tombs because robbers knew that great riches—gold and other jewels—were buried with their owners. Almost all of the burial chambers were vandalized over the years. Tut's claim to fame rests not on any accomplishments made while he was alive, but rather on the fact that his tomb was found nearly intact.

Tut's tomb was discovered by Howard Carter, a British Egyptologist who searched for years before he found it in 1922, and Lord Carnarvon, who financed the expedition. When the excavation team unearthed the door to the burial chamber, the original seal was in place and unbroken, and they knew they had made a remarkable discovery. Inside, in addition to the household items, they found a red sandstone sarcophagus, which held three other coffins. Tut's mummy was discovered inside the third, with its head protected by the gold mask that has become famous worldwide. The rest of the mummy was in poor condition. His preserved internal organs were found in four canopic jars within an alabaster chest in a separate room.

King Tut's treasures are kept in the Egyptian Museum in Cairo, the country's capital, but they regularly travel to other museums around the world and have been viewed by millions. The discovery of his tomb was one of the most important finds among all the treasures of Ancient Egypt, proving that the stories and legends of unbelievable riches were true, even though no other tombs had ever been found with their treasures intact.

Shortly after the discovery of Tut's tomb, several members of the archaeological group—including Carnarvon—died suddenly, and some say suspiciously. These untimely deaths resurrected the legend of the curse of the pharaohs, which stated that whoever disturbed a pharaoh's tomb would die. This curse can be found written in and around many of the kings' tombs. Near Tut's tomb, hieroglyphs proclaim, "Death shall come on swift wings to him who disturbs the peace of the king." This curse was even the basis for some recent movies made about mummies, pharaohs, and curses. Yet, some modern scientists theorize that mold—which may have accumulated within the darkness of the sealed tombs—had something to do with any deaths that occurred shortly after they were opened.

Tut's tomb may have been the last royal tomb in the Valley of the Kings to be discovered, but some researchers believe that others remain hidden. Unfortunately, the tombs of Akhenaten and Nefertiti have not yet been discovered with any certainty.

7

The Mysterious Queen Nefertiti

BY ALMOST ANY STANDARD, QUEEN NEFERTITI WAS A STRIKINGLY BEAUTIFUL woman. With a narrow face set atop a long, swan-like neck, large dark eyes, full red lips, and a creamy complexion, she was recognized during her lifetime as one of the most beautiful women of her day. Mere appearance is not everything, however, and Nefertiti also had a regal bearing—one that seemed to convey self-confidence and perhaps even a sense that she was a born leader.

What the world knows today about Queen Nefertiti is fairly limited. We would know even less if not for a fortunate accident in 1912. A poor woman, out digging in a field, came across some pottery. She reported the find, and archaeological crews descended on the spot. Following an excavation by German archaeologists, a village was uncovered that had never been heard of before. This village eventually expanded to contain an entire city—the city of Amarna. What we have learned about Amarna and those who ruled it has offered a whole new perspective of our view of Ancient Egypt. Before this discovery, only the most highly educated Egyptologists knew about Nefertiti. This lack of common knowledge was not surprising, considering that the city in which she lived as queen was partially destroyed and what remained had been hidden for centuries.

Scholars today theorize that Nefertiti and her husband, the Pharaoh Akhenaten, had many enemies who tried to obliterate as much evidence of their lives as they could. Nefertiti was apparently an uncommonly powerful queen; some think she was really the guiding force behind the throne. Early scenes carved in Aten's temple at Karnak show her posed like a warrior king, holding her enemies by their hair. She is often depicted as taking an active role in the religious life of the country, even serving as a priestess. She appears in several paintings taking part in worship and making offerings to Aten. Prime among those who hated her because of her influence were the priests who had held so much power before she and Akhenaten came to the throne. They were not happy about losing their jobs when the gods they served were banned by the royal couple, and it would have been easy to get the common folk angry about the changes too. Some scholars even think her enemies may have killed her.

NEFERTITI'S BUST

Fortunately, the shifting desert sands that covered Amarna hid many beautiful and precious objects from grave robbers and other thieves, so much survived for us to study today. Perhaps one of the most beautiful pieces of artwork from this period of Egyptian history is the carved limestone bust of Nefertiti. As scientists dug through the city's remains, they discovered the workshop of a sculptor named Thutmose, the official sculptor for the royal court at Armana. There, among the unidentifiable

Nefertiti, meaning "a beautiful woman has arrived," lived up to her name when archaeologists discovered a centuries-old bust created in her image. Carved from limestone and painted, the bust stirred up a great amount of excitement. However, archaeologists could not locate Nefertiti's mummy and concluded that it was either destroyed by her enemies or hidden away by those loyal to her.

ruins, the nearly complete bust of Nefertiti was unearthed. The fact that the bust of this beautiful woman had survived the wreckage around it, and centuries of being covered by sand, was remarkable. Limestone is a sedimentary stone—usually almost pure white and often found in caves, rivers, or the ocean—that forms from the skeletons of tiny animals and fish. The bust was meticulously carved, with every little detail in place, and then was painted in rich colors, which gave Nefertiti's face a café au lait tone and her headdress a deep, sky blue.

Nefertiti's sculpture is considered one of the most beautiful busts ever created. A bust is a carved representation of a person's head and shoulders, and hers is said to represent the "ideal" woman—at least according to the standards of Ancient Egypt. The bust has been dated to the year 1345 B.C., making it more than 3,200 years old, and it has been on display in the Egyptian Museum in Berlin, Germany, since 1924. Nefertiti's image has been reproduced countless times around the world, for many different reasons—it even appears on paper money. Perhaps she seems so familiar in part because her image is used and displayed so frequently. The fact that no royal tomb or any reference to a royal burial has been found for Nefertiti supports the theories that she was hated by many of her subjects, who would not have wanted to dignify her even in death. Although some jewelry with her cartouche was found near the royal tomb at Amarna, there is no proof that she was buried there. Possessing great beauty, charm, and power as she ruled alongside her husband, she vanished seemingly without a trace. She truly is among the most mysterious "famous" people who ever lived.

WHAT DO WE KNOW?

The name Nefertiti means, roughly, "the beauty (or beautiful woman) who has come." She was the great royal wife of Pharaoh Amenhotep IV, who later changed his name to Akhenaten in honor of the sun-disk god, Aten. Akhenaten had at least two other wives—Kiya (the mother of Tutenkhamen) and Ankhesenpaten. Much later, it is believed that Akhenaten took his eldest daughter by Nefertiti, Meritaten, as a third wife.

Nefertiti was his primary wife, and the most important. The two ruled side by side, first in Thebes, and then for about 12 more years after moving the court to Amarna. Many references to Nefertiti have been found among Amarna's ruins, including inscriptions that list various names and descriptions for the queen: Heiress, Great of Favor, Possessed of Charm, Exuding Happiness, Mistress of Sweetness, Beloved One, Soothing the King's Heart in His House, Soft-Spoken in All, Mistress of Upper and Lower Egypt, Great King's Wife, Whom He Loves, and Lady of the Two Lands.

Names, bloodlines, and years of the various pharaohs' reigns are confusing, and—as with much of the information

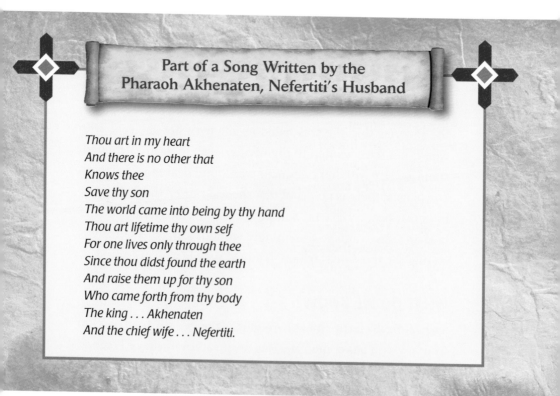

Part of a Song Written by the Pharaoh Akhenaten, Nefertiti's Husband

Thou art in my heart
And there is no other that
Knows thee
Save thy son
The world came into being by thy hand
Thou art lifetime thy own self
For one lives only through thee
Since thou didst found the earth
And raise them up for thy son
Who came forth from thy body
The king . . . Akhenaten
And the chief wife . . . Nefertiti.

about Nefertiti—there are those who propose many different theories. In approximately the fourteenth year of Akhenaten's rule, references to Nefertiti suddenly stopped. About this same time, a co-regent by the name of Smenkhkare appeared to rule with Akhenaten and continued to rule briefly after his death, until Akhenaten's son, Tutenkhaman, took the throne. Some Egyptologists believe that Smenkhkare was actually Nefertiti disguised as a man. Others believe that she might have ruled the country briefly after her husband died, using the name Neferneferuaten (which can mean "The Aten is radiant because the beautiful one is come"). Still others believe that Smenkhkare was one of Akhenaten's sons by a lesser wife, and that Nefertiti acted as his co-regent under the name Neferneferuaten. It may be that Nefertiti's oldest child, Meritaten, took over as great royal wife while her mother served as king. We most likely will never know which theory is correct, if any.

At about this time, Nefertiti appears in a painted scene of another daughter's burial. Her second child apparently died in childbirth, and the scene depicts a grieving Nefertiti and Akhenaten standing near her bed, while a nurse stands nearby holding a baby. This is the last depiction of Nefertiti as herself, Akhenaten's queen.

Clues to her life are found among the writings and paintings found on walls, shards of pottery, and tombs in the Amarna excavation, and in records left by the court's scribes. Because the words and pictures of her cease abruptly near the end of her husband's reign, it has been difficult for Egyptologists to piece together any reliably accurate histories of Nefertiti. Did she leave Amarna voluntarily? Was she killed? Did she go into hiding and then resurface when her husband died, and did she then rule in his place? Most likely, the answers to these questions will never be answered completely. No one knows when Nefertiti died, or from what. Whenever such a mystery surrounds someone who generates so much public interest, people tend to speculate and come up with various theories.

After the discovery of Nefertiti's bust, archaeologists began to find and decipher hieroglyphics, pottery, and tombs that provided more information about the queen's life. Details of her role after the death of Akhenaten, however, are non-existent. It is believed that her enemies and later Egyptian leaders destroyed much of her legacy and vandalized her tomb, even chiseling out her cartouche *(above)*.

One of the most prominent of these is that Nefertiti was murdered by the priests who had lost their power when Akhenetan replaced their gods with his god, Aten. Others think that she may have been kidnapped and hidden away by the court officials who also saw some of their power and prestige deteriorate because of her influence.

Even Nefertiti's origins remain shrouded in mystery. The bust's features are, in some ways, more like those of a European woman than an Egyptian woman, although some skeptics suggest that the German scientist who discovered the bust may have altered it to appear more beautiful by German standards of 1912. Improved forensic technologies have allowed scientists to recreate her features around the skull of a mummy that some believe to be Nefertiti's, although the resulting model does not answer any questions definitively.

Some researchers believe that Nefertiti was born into Egyptian royalty, but most researchers who have studied this era tend to believe that she was the daughter of a high government official, and that she caught the eye of Prince Amenhotep IV (who later changed his name to Akhenaten). Her marriage would have improved the status of everyone in her family. Some think that her father was an official named Ay, and that he was possibly Akhenaten's uncle (his mother's brother). Ay went on to rule as pharaoh after King Tutenkhamen died. Some even speculate that Ay may have been part of a conspiracy to murder the young king, so he could ascend to the throne. We do not know who Nefertiti's mother was, but writings indicate that Nefertiti was raised by another one of Ay's wives, Tey. It is possible that Nefertiti's mother died in childbirth.

ROYAL DEPICTIONS

Nefertiti and Akhenaten had six daughters, and many scenes that depict their seemingly happy family life have been unearthed. Their daughters' names, in descending order of birth, were Meritaten, Meketaten, Ankhenspaaten, Neferneferuaten, Neferneferure, and Setepenre. A depiction of a close marital relationship, especially within the royal family, was a rarity in Ancient Egypt. Royal families usually were shown in stiff portrait poses—not playing and interacting in affectionate ways. Paintings, however, show Pharaoh Akhenaten with his arm around his wife and playing with his daughters. Reliefs portray the two riding in a chariot, with her sitting on his lap.

Other, more posed paintings and sculptures have been found that depict the king and queen in more formal settings. Yet even these staged scenes are different from other Egyptian depictions of royal families because they are so realistic.

Generally, Egyptian sculptors would carve the king with a serious expression and perfect features, but Akhenaten was shown as having somewhat irregular features, including a high forehead and long nose. In full-length paintings, he was depicted as stocky, with a potbelly. As mentioned previously, some people believe he may have had a disease that resulted in physical deformities. He did not appear to be a very handsome man, by standards of the day. Nefertiti, on the other hand, was slender when shown at full length. It was common to portray the woman as being shorter than the man, so it is unclear whether she was shorter than her husband or if the artists merely depicted her that way.

In 2003, a *USA Today* article by Tim Friend discussed two specialists who had reconstructed a face around an Ancient Egyptian mummy. The specialists' usual jobs were to reconstruct faces on skulls from murder cases in which the victim's identity was unknown. Friend wrote that the mummy had been identified by British Egyptologist Joann Fletcher, Ph.D., as belonging to Nefertiti, but the specialists had not known this before they began their work. Damian Schofield from England's Nottingham University and Martin Evison of Sheffield University built a 3-D computer "mesh" of the skull, added material to give the face its form, and brought in a graphic artist to add the skin, eyes, lips, and crown.

Some believe that this re-creation is eerily similar to the painted bust found in the sculptor's workshop in Amarna, and Fletcher has continued her attempts to prove further that this mummy is indeed the beautiful Egyptian queen. Dr. Fletcher said of the reconstruction, "I was bowled over by it, to be honest. The face is that of a very strong individual indeed. She has such a beautiful profile. She is stunning."

It has thus far been impossible to determine how old Nefertiti was at the time she posed for the now-famous bust, but the director of the Egyptian Museum in Berlin, Dietrich Wildung, recently reported that he believes she was older than 30, as was previously assumed. He closely examined the bust using a different type of light and a CT scan, and discovered that the sculptor had added gypsum around Nefertiti's eyes and cheeks, which created fine lines and slight puffiness. Other scholars believe that Nefertiti was made to look older after her mother-in-law died, when Nefertiti would have taken over the role of wise older woman of the court. The perfection of Nefertiti's bust is marred by a missing left eye, which may have been left out on purpose. Director Wildung suggests that the sculptor was also an instructor, and that he was trying to teach his students the proper alignment and placement for a realistic eye in a bust. He also believes that the bust was a model to be used for the painting of the queen's official portrait.

We will never know every detail of Nefertiti's life. Yet, somehow, the mystery surrounding her only serves to make her that much more intriguing.

8

Could This
Be Nefertiti?

OVER THE COURSE OF THE PAST COUPLE YEARS, BRITISH EGYPTOLOGIST
Joann Fletcher has gone public with a theory that has astounded
the archaeological world. She believes that she has identified
the mummy of Nefertiti.

When the tomb of Amenhotep II, King Tut's great-
grandfather, was excavated in 1898 outside of Thebes, the pharaoh was found—along with 11 other mummies—in a sealed
chamber. Three of those 11 were left in place in the tomb
because of their poor condition. One of those mummies was
a young woman who became known as the "Younger Woman";
the second was an older woman with thick, auburn hair, and the
third was the body of a young boy. In June 2002, Dr. Fletcher
visited the excavation site and identified several qualities of the

Younger Woman mummy that led her to believe it was Nefertiti: She had a double-pierced ear (a symbol of royalty), a shaved head, and an impression in her skull of the band that royals wore around their foreheads.

Other details strengthened her belief. The mummy was terribly mutilated; its right arm had been torn off and was found nearby. The elbow was bent and its fingers were closed, as if they had been holding something—perhaps a royal scepter? Its skull had a large hole in it and the face had been gouged, so that the mouth and one cheek were missing. The chest also had been cut.

As Dr. Fletcher sees it, several facts further support her claim. Grave robbers knew that jewels often were placed inside the body's cavities after internal organs were removed during the mummification process. Often the rich and royal dead were buried wearing jewelry, so the damage to this mummy's chest may have been inflicted during the course of a robbery. Furthermore, Ancient Egyptians believed that, as part of the afterlife, they were given the "breath of life." Destroying this mummy's mouth would have been a way to ensure that she was unable to receive that breath, keeping her from living on in the next world. Dr. Fletcher believes that whoever damaged the mummy knew that it was Nefertiti and mutilated it out of hatred. The Ancient Egyptians believed that speaking a dead person's name gave him or her life again, after death; by removing items that would help identify Nefertiti, whoever damaged the mummy ensured that no one would be able to speak her name, because they would not know her identity.

According to Maryalice Yakutchik on discovery.com, Dr. Fletcher also came across an unlabeled wig in the Egyptian Museum at Cairo while working on a thesis about hair. She discovered that the hairpiece came from the tomb known as KV35, discovered in 1898 by Victor Loret. Loret wrote that he had found a hairpiece in a side chamber that held a bald mummy with a profile strikingly similar to the bust of Nefertiti. The hair

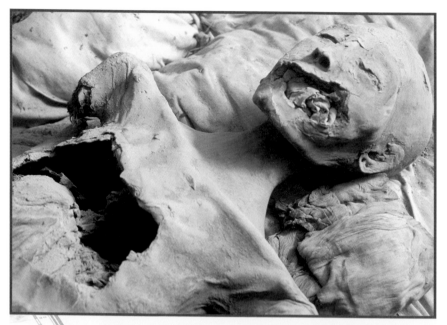

In 2001, Dr. Joann Fletcher announced her suspicion that one of the female mummies discovered in Akhenaten's tomb was Nefertiti. Although she has no definitive evidence to prove her case, Fletcher believes the face of the mummy is an important clue to its identity. Fletcher hypothesizes the face was damaged by enemies of the queen, possibly even the new leaders of the kingdom, to prevent her from traveling on to the afterlife.

in the wig was short, which was similar to the style of royal women of Amarna during the eighteenth dynasty.

Dr. Fletcher's fellow Egyptologists are not all convinced that the Younger Woman mummy is actually the ancient queen, although they do agree that the mummy dates from the late eighteenth dynasty and probably was a member of the royal family. Dr. Fletcher concedes that, unless the mummy were to sit up and state that she is Nefertiti, there is likely no way to positively identify her.

As for the older woman's mummy, Dr. Fletcher believes that she may be Queen Tiye—head wife of Amenhotep III,

Akhenaten's mother, and Nefertiti's mother-in-law. Her features are similar to a painting of Queen Tiye's mother, and, in the 1970s, a team of archaeologists from America and Egypt first proposed that she was Tiye. The young boy discovered with the two women was only about 10 years old, and he was found positioned between them. He had pierced ears, a shaved head, and the sidelock hair worn by most young boys of the day. His features are similar to the older mummy, and Dr. Fletcher speculates that he is Tiye's son, Tuthmosis.

Dr. Fletcher has been using the most up-to-date technology to examine the mummies, including a form of X-rays that indicate that the feet of all three mummies were damaged. Damaging the feet might keep the dead person from walking into the afterlife. She believes that the bodies were intentionally mutilated, but many questions remain unanswered.

CONCLUSION

Nefertiti was a beautiful and powerful woman of Ancient Egypt. She married a pharaoh who may have been forgotten by history altogether, except for his status as the "heretic king" who completely changed the way his country worshiped. Akhenaten's decree that Egyptians should no longer worship hundreds of gods, as they had for thousands of years, was not widely accepted. The new, monotheistic religion instituted by Akhenaten and Queen Nefertiti was the first known religion of its kind. They established a new city in which to worship their god, Aten, in peace, but Akhenaten lived there only about 13 or 14 years before he died. All traces of Nefertiti had already disappeared three years before his death. Within a few years, their capital city, Amarna, was deserted and later almost completely destroyed. King Akhenaten's son, King Tutenkhamen, established his palace back in Thebes and lived out his short life there.

Ancient Egypt has a very long, colorful, and confusing history. Egyptologists continue to make new discoveries and dig

In spite of all the damage done to the mummy, Dr. Joann Fletcher was able to recreate a portrait using X-rays and computer technology. The portrait *(above)* bears a striking resemblance to Nefertiti's bust, and may be one of the few accurate depictions in existence of this strong, beautiful monarch.

deeper into its past, proposing various theories along the way. We do have some concrete knowledge of this country and its people, thanks to significant discoveries such as the Rosetta Stone and King Tut's tomb. However, there are many more mysteries that may forever remain uncovered.

CHRONOLOGY

◆ ◆ ◆

7000 B.C. (approx.)   People begin to settle in the Nile Valley.

3400 B.C. (approx.)   A powerful king unites the upper and lower regions of Ancient Egypt.

2686–2160 B.C.   The Old Kingdom, which includes the third through sixth dynasties of Ancient Egypt; characterized by pharaohs who wield nearly complete power over their subjects and are seen as gods as well as kings; the construction of the pyramids begins.

c. 2540 B.C.   The Great Pyramid of Giza, one of the seven wonders of the ancient world, is built as the tomb of King Khufu.

2055–1650 B.C.   The Middle Kingdom, which begins during the eleventh dynasty and continues through the end of the thirteenth; priests and local officials grow in power and prestige; agriculture increases along the Nile River.

1570–1070 B.C.   The New Kingdom, which includes the Amarna Period and the eighteenth through twentieth dynasties; some of the most famous pharaohs rule during this time, including Akhenaten, Tutenkhamen, Seti, and Ramses.

1350–1334 B.C.   The Pharaoh Akhenaten, Nefertiti's husband, reigns for 17 years; early in his rule, he moves the capital from Thebes to Amarna, starting two decades of controversy over changes in religion and art.

1334 B.C. Nefertiti's stepson, King Tut, rules for approximately 10 years, until his death at age 19.

333 B.C. Alexander the Great invades Egypt, and the Macedonians rule until about 31 B.C.

1500s Egypt is ruled for about 300 years by the Ottoman Turks.

1700 Egypt becomes a part of the British Empire.

1798 Napolean invades from France; he is turned back by 1801 by the British and the Turks.

1859–1869 The Suez Canal is built.

1912 The lost city of Amarna—built by Nefertiti's husband, Pharaoh Akhenaten, as a tribute to the sun god, Aten—is unearthed by German archaeologists; the now-famous bust of Queen Nefertiti is discovered in the ruins of a sculptor's workshop.

1922 Egypt gains partial independence, and Fu'ad I becomes its king; the tomb of King Tut is discovered in the Valley of the Kings, on the western shore of the Nile River in southern Egypt, by British Egyptologist Howard Carter and financier Lord Carnarvon.

1948 Egypt joins with Iraq, Jordan, and Syria to attack the newly formed state of Israel.

1952 Egypt gains full independence from Great Britain; Gamal Abdel Nasser, leader of the revolution, becomes its first president.

1981 Mohammed Hosni Mubarak becomes president of the republic of Egypt.

1980s Excavation is completed on the tomb of Pharaoh Ramses VI, sixth king of the twentieth dynasty, who reigned from about 1133 to 1125 B.C.

BIBLIOGRAPHY

◆ ◆ ◆

Asimov, Isaac. *The Egyptians.* Boston: Houghton Mifflin, 1967.

Frank, Nicole, and Susan L. Wilson. *Welcome to Egypt.* Milwaukee, Wis.: Gareth Stevens Publishing, 2000.

Friend, Tim. "Could This Be the Profile of a Queen?" *USA Today.* Available online. URL: www.usatoday.com/news/science/2003–08–12-nefertiti-usat_x.htm.

Harris, Geraldine. *Ancient Egypt: Cultural Atlas for Young People.* New York, NY: Facts on File, 2003.

Hart, George. *Ancient Egypt.* New York: Dorling Kindersley, 2000.

Malek, Jaromir. *Cradles of Civilization: Egypt.* Norman: University of Oklahoma Press, 1993.

Meltzer, Milton. *In the Days of the Pharaohs: A Look at Ancient Egypt.* New York: Franklin Watts, 2001.

FURTHER READING

◆ ◆ ◆

Fairservis, Jr., Walter. *Egypt, Gift of the Nile: Life Under the Pharaohs.* New York: Macmillan, 1963.

Fletcher, Joann. *The Search for Nefertiti: The True Story of an Amazing Discovery.* New York: HarperCollins, 2004.

Hawass, Zahi A., and Sandro Vannini. *The Royal Tombs of Egypt.* London: Thames & Hudson, 2006.

McNeill, Sarah. *Ancient Egyptian People.* Brookfield, Conn.: Millbrook Press, 1997.

Wallis Budge, E.A. *The Egyptian Book of the Dead: The Papyrus of Ani in the British Museum.* New York: Dover, 1967.

WEB SITES

Guide to travel in Egypt:
www.touregypt.net/

Guide to Egyptology online:
www.egyptologyonline.com
www.seaworld.org/egypt/egypt.html
www.globalfriends.com/html/world_tour/Eypt/Egypt.htm
www.Discovery.com

PHOTO CREDITS

◆ ◆ ◆

INDEX

◆ ◆ ◆

A

action, leadership and, 8
A.D. time, 13–15
adoption, 34
afterlife
    mummification and, 53
    religion and, 48–50
Age of the Pyramids, overview
    of, 13–15
agriculture, 25–27, 35
Ahhotep, 64
Ahmose, 64
Akhenaten
    art and, 75
    construction of Amarna
      by, 13
    mother of, 63–64
    overview of, 69–73
    paintings of, 87–88
    polygamy and, 21
    relationship with, 16–17
    religion and, 17–20, 73–74
    song written by, 84
    wives of, 83–84
Alexander the Great, 25
Amarna
    architecture in, 74–75
    art and, 75
    discovery of by German
      archaeologists, 13, 80–81

New Kingdom and, 15
    overview of, 68–69
    religion and, 18–20
Amenhotep III
    Akhenaten and, 69
    Tiye and, 64
    tomb of, 90–93
Amenhotep IV. *See* Akhenaten
American Commonwealth, The
    (Bryce), 9
amulets, 38
Amun-Ra
    creation stories and, 50
    Karnak and, 30–31
    overview of, 56–57, 73
    Thebes and, 69
Ancient Egypt (Hart), 50
animals, 24, 28, 53–54, 57
Ankhesenamun, 76
Ankhesenpaten, 84, 87
Anubis, 57
Arabic, as official language, 26
architecture, in Amarna,
    74–75
art. *See also* bust of Nefertiti
    Amarna Period and, 18
    changes in, 75
    daily life and, 35
    great works of, 28–29
assessor gods, 50
astronomy, 56

Aten
    Akhenaten and, 13,
        18–20
    changes of Nefertiti and,
        73–74
    Nefertiti as goddess to, 56
    offerings to, 16
Ay, 70, 87

B

barley, 41–42
Bastet, 28, 56
B.C. time, 13–15
beads, Nefer, 13, 43
beauty, 42–43, 80–83
Bes, 57
black land, 27
board games, 37
"Boy King." *See* Tutenkhamen
    (King Tut)
bread, 41–42
Bryce, James, 9
burials, royal, 61–63
bust of Nefertiti
    age when posing for, 89
    description of, 12–13
    mysteries surrounding, 21,
        86–87
    Nefer beads and, 43
    overview of, 81–83

C

Cairo, 26, 78
camels, 60
Carnarvon, Lord, 78
Carter, Howard, 78
cats, 28, 53–54, 57
cedar wood, 35
chariots, 60
children, views on, 34
Christ, Jesus, A.D., B.C., and,
    13–15
Churchill, Winston, 7

class structure
    lifestyle differences and,
        37–38
    mummification and, 53
    overview of, 33–34
Cleopatra VII, 25, 66
clothing, 42–43, 61–63
Constasino, Mario, 7
co-regents, 63
creation stories, 49–50
crocodiles, 28, 37, 40
crowns, 26
cucumbers, 42
curse of King Tut's tomb, 78–79

D

dates, 42
daughters of Nefertiti and
    Akhenaten, 87–88
Days of the Pharaohs, In the
    (Meltzer), 51
death, religion and, 48–50
death of Nefertiti, lack of knowl-
    edge about, 85–86
deformities, 70–72, 88
dehydration, mummification
    and, 51
Democracy, leadership and,
    9–10
Democracy in America (de
    Tocqueville), 9–10
demotic, 46, 72
deserts, 28
determinism, historical, 6–7
Devourer of the Dead, 50
diet of Egyptians, 26, 41–42
Discovery Channel documen-
    tary, 23
diseases, 38
divorce, 34–36
Djoser (Pharaoh), 15, 29
documentaries, 23
donkeys, 60
Duat, 48

E

ebony wood, 35
education, 35, 36–37, 63
Egypt
    in ancient times, 26–28
    art of, 18, 28–29
    clothing, beauty, fashion and,
        42–43
    diet and, 41–42
    family life in, 34–38
    homes of, 40–41
    Karnak and, 30–31, 56, 81
    medicine in, 38–40
    overview of everyday life in,
        33–34
    people of, 25–26
    physical description of,
        24–25
    religion and, 17–20, 47–58
    scribes, hieroglyphics and,
        43–46
    special occasions of, 42
    three kingdoms of, 13–16
    Valley of the Kings and, 30,
        32, 77–79
Egyptian Museum, 78, 83, 89
Egyptology, defined, 23
El-Amarna
    architecture in, 74–75
    art and, 75
    discovery of by German
        archaeologists, 13, 80–81
    New Kingdom and, 15
    overview of, 68–69
    religion and, 18–20
embalming, 51, 57
emmer, 41–42
enemies of Nefertiti, 81
equality, leadership and, 9–10
Ethiopia, Nile River and, 24
eulogy to Nefertiti, 20
Evison, Martin, 88
eye, missing, 89
eye shadow, 42–43

F

facial reconstruction, 88
farming, 25–27, 35
fashion, 42–43
Federalist Papers, 10
feet, damaged, 93
fertility, 42
figs, 42
fish, 42
flax, 42
Fletcher, Joann, 88, 90–93
flooding, Nile River and, 24,
    26–27
followers, leadership and, 8
food of Egyptians, 26, 41–42
foul (boiled fava beans), 26
freedom, determinism vs., 7
Friend, Tim, 88

G

galena, 42–43
games, 37, 42
gender roles, 63–66
Giza, Great Pyramid at, 15, 29, 61
gods. *See also* polytheism
    changing views of, 18, 73–74
    pharaohs as, 54–56
    temples and, 54
gourds, 42
grave robbery, 77–78, 91
Great Britain, 25
Great Pyramid at Giza, 15, 29, 61
"Great Royal Wife" title, 63
Great Sphinx, 28–29, 66

H

hair, 43, 91–92
Hall of the Two Truths, 48–49
Hamilton, Alexander, 10
Hart, George, 50
Hatshepsut, 64–66
hawks, 57
headdresses, 62–63, 83

heretic king, 73. *See also*
   Akhenaten
hieratic, 46
hieroglyphics, 18, 31,
   43–46, 72
hippos, 28
historical determinism, 6–7
Hitler, Adolf, 7
homes of Egypt, 40–41
Horemheb, 45, 70
Horus, 17, 57
humans, portrayal of, 30

I

ibis, 50, 56
individuals, leadership and, 6
infant mortality rate, 34
inheritance, 35, 63
iron oxide, 43
irrigation ditches, 25–26
Isis, 17

J

James, William, 7–8
jewelry
   everyday life and, 43
   family life and, 35
   King Tut's tomb and,
      76–78
   mummies and, 52
   royalty and, 62–63
justice, importance of, 60

K

Karnak, 30–31, 56, 81
Keynes, John Maynard, 8
Khufu, 15, 29, 61
kidnapping theory, 86
King Tut. *See* Tutenkhamen
Kiya, Akhenaten and, 17,
   76, 84
kohl, 43

L

land ownership, 34, 35–36
languages, 72
languages of Egypt, 26
Leadership, Schlesinger on, 6–11
Lenin, Vladimir, 7
Libya, as neighbor of Egypt, 24
limestone, 83
Lincoln, Abraham, 11
lions, 57
litters, 60
location of Egypt, 24
Loret, Victor, 91
Lower Egypt, 26, 61
Luxor, 30, 32, 56–57

M

Ma'at, 60
magic, medicine and, 38–40
Marfan syndrome, 70–72
marriage
   family life and, 34–35
   polygamy and, 21
   record-keeping and, 44
   royalty and, 63
Marxism, 7
mathematics, scribes and, 44
medicine, overview of, 38–40
Mediterranean Sea, 24
Meketaten, 87
melons, 42
Meltzer, Milton, 51
Memphis, Old Kingdom and, 15
Meritaten, 84, 87
metalworking, 35
Middle Kingdom, overview of, 15
military, 63, 70, 72
monotheism, 17–20, 73–74
moral code, 37, 60
mortality rates, 34, 47
movies, 23
Mubarak, Mohammed Hosni,
   16, 25

mummies
    cats and, 28
    facial reconstruction and, 88
    King Tut's treasures and, 78
    of Nefertiti, 88, 90–93
    overview of, 51–54
murder theory, 86
mutilation, mummies and, 91
mysteries surrounding Nefertiti,
    21–22, 80–89

N

names, importance of, 57–58, 66
Napoleonic Wars, 6–7
Nasser, Gamal Abdel, 25
natron, 52
Nazism, 7
nefer beads, 13, 43
Neferneferuaten, 85, 87
Neferneferure, 87
Nekhbet, 63
New Kingdom, 15, 32
Niebuhr, Reinhold, 10
Nile River
    agriculture and, 26–27
    construction of houses from
        mud of, 40–41
    diet and, 41–42
    mens' roles and, 35
    overview of, 24
Nitocris, 64
nomes, 57, 59
Nubia, 64, 70

O

oases, overview of, 24–25
obelisks, 31
Old Kingdom, overview of,
    13–15
order, importance of, 60
origins of Nefertiti, lack of
    knowledge about, 86–87
Osiris, 17, 50, 56–57

ostraca, 44
Ottoman Empire, 15, 25

P

paintings, 30, 85, 87–88
palaces, 20, 60, 74
palettes, 46
papermaking, 40
papyrus, 40, 44
Parcheesi, 37
Pepy II, 64, 66
Persia, 25
Persians, 15
pets, mummification of, 53–54
pharaohs. See also specific
    pharaohs
    crowns of, 26
    as gods, 54–56
    kingdoms of Egypt and,
        13–16
    mummification and, 53
    overview of, 59–60
    people of Egypt and, 25
piercings, 91
pith, papyrus and, 40
polygamy, 21, 63, 66
polytheism, 17, 47, 76
pottery, 35
power of Nefertiti, overview of,
    16–17
pyramids, 15, 29–30. See also
    specific pyramids

R

Ra, 18, 56–57, 73
race, determinism and, 7
Ramses, 15
Ramses II, 66
Ramses VI (King), tomb of, 32
reconstruction, facial, 88
red land, 28
Red Sea, location of Egypt and,
    24, 28

reeks, 15
religion
    afterlife and, 48–50
    Akhenaten and, 17–20
    education and, 37
    gods, goddesses and,
        56–58
    mummification and, 51–54
    overview of, 47–48
    pharaohs and, 54–56
    temples and, 54
    Thebes and, 69
    Tutenkhamen and, 76
rituals, mummification and, 53
robbery, grave, 77–78, 91
Romans, 15, 25
Roosevelt, Franklin D., 7
Rosetta Stone, 72, 95
royalty. See also pharaohs
    burials and, 61–63
    overview of, 59–60
    women and, 63–66

S

Sahara Desert, 27–28, 72
sandals, 43
sarcophaguses, 78
scepters, 62
Schofield, Damian, 88
scribes, 34, 37, 43–46. See also
    hieroglyphics
scrolls, afterworld and, 48
sculpture, 88. See also bust of
    Nefertiti
seasons of Egypt, 24
Set, 17
Setepenre, 87
Seti, New Kingdom and, 15
seven wonders of the ancient
    world, 29
shaduf, 25–26
slavery, 29, 60
Smenkhkare, 16, 85
"Snake" game, 37

snakes, 48
Sobeknefru, 64
Sphinx, 28–29, 66
Step Pyramid, 29
Sudan, as neighbor of Egypt, 24
sun god (Ra), 18, 56–57, 73
Sycamore trees, 57

T

taxes, scribes and, 44
temples
    Amarna and, 74
    building of, 20, 29–31, 35
    religion and, 54
Tey, 87
Thebes, 30–31, 32, 69, 73
Thoth, 50, 56
Thutmose (sculptor), 21, 81
Thutmose IV (King), 29
time, designations of, 13–15
Tiye (Queen), 63–64, 69–70,
    92–93
t'miya (fried chickpeas and
    wheat), 26
Tocqueville, Alexis de, 9–10, 11
Tolstoy, Leo, 6–7
tombs
    Amarna and, 74–75
    building of, 35
    lack of knowledge about, 32
    mummy of Nefertiti and, 88,
        90–93
    royalty and, 60, 61
    Tutenkhamen and, 32, 61, 67,
        78–79
travel, methods of, 60
truth, importance of, 60
Turks, 15, 25
Tutenkhamen (King Tut)
    New Kingdom and, 15
    overview of, 66–67, 75–79
    parentage of, 17, 66
    Sphinx and, 29
    tomb of, 32, 61, 67, 78–79

Tuthmose, 70
Tuthmosis IV, 66, 93

U

underworld, 48, 56–57
Upper Egypt, 26, 61

V

Valley of the Kings, 30, 32, 77–79

W

wadis (riverbeds), 28
Wadjet, 63
War and Peace (Tolstoy), 6–7

Waters of Chaos, 49–50
wigs, 43, 91–92
wildlife of Egypt, 24, 28
Wildung, Dietrich, 89
wills, 44
Wilson, Woodrow, 8
wine, 42
women, royalty and, 63–66
woodworking, 35

Y

Yakutchik, Maryalice, 91

Z

Zangara, Guiseppe, 7

ABOUT THE AUTHORS

◆ ◆ ◆

BRENDA LANGE has been a journalist, author, and public relations professional for 20 years. In addition to her work with Chelsea House—this is her sixth book for young adults—she has written for newspapers, magazines, trade publications, and performed public relations functions for a diverse clientele. Brenda is a member of ASJA and SPJ and lives and works in Doylestown, Pennsylvania. Her Web site is www.brendalange.com.

ARTHUR SCHLESINGER, JR. is remembered as the leading American historian of our time. He won the Pulitzer Prize for his books *The Age of Jackson* (1945) and *A Thousand Days* (1965), which also won the National Book Award. Schlesinger was the Albert Schweitzer Professor of the Humanities at the City University of New York and was involved in several other Chelsea House projects, including the series *Revolutionary War Leaders*, *Colonial Leaders*, and *Your Government*.